FEED THE BEAR

Roy Aitken is one of Scotland's most popular footballers of all time. He relates to the fans. Whether in a Celtic or Scotland jersey, he is loved on the terraces and in the stands because of his honest thrusting skills. When he is on the ball the adoring chant invariably goes up: "Feed the Bear!". It is meant in the nicest way.

In a career which began in 1975 and in a host of matches at home and abroad for club and country, Roy Aitken has amassed a wealth of experience and anecdotes. In *FEED THE BEAR!* Aitken gives his views on the different approaches of managers Jock Stein, Billy McNeill and David Hay; talks of the awful day he was sent off in the Scottish Cup final at Hampden; discloses what went on behind the scenes at the World Cup in Mexico; and considers the effect Rangers' big cash plunge has had on Celtic. It is a book football fans will not want to miss. As Celtic approach their centenary celebrations, Roy Aitken, Celtic and Scotland captain, tells his story the way he plays — forcefully and fairly.

FEED THE BEAR

ROY AITKEN'S OWN STORY

Roy Aitken
with
Alex Cameron

MAINSTREAM
PUBLISHING

First published in Great Britain in 1987 by
MAINSTREAM PUBLISHING COMPANY (EDINBURGH) LTD
7 Albany Street
Edinburgh EH1 3UG

ISBN 1 85158 073 5 (cloth)
ISBN 1 85158 074 3 (paper)

British Library Cataloguing in Publication Data

Aitken, Roy
Feed the bear : the Roy Aitken story.
1. Aitken, Roy 2. Soccer players——
Scotland——Biography
I. Title II. Cameron, Alex
796.334'092'4 GV942.7.A3

ISBN 1-85158-073-5
ISBN 1-85158-074-3 Pbk

Typeset in Baskerville by Pulse Origination, Edinburgh.
Printed in Great Britain by Billing & Sons, Worcester.

Contents

CELTIC FOOTBALL CLUB 1888

FOREWORD

In 1988 Celtic celebrate the centenary of the club and it is absolutely right and fitting that Roy Aitken is captain of the team as this milestone in our history emerges.

Roy is the player who is loved by the legions of Celtic fans and highly respected by opponents and opposition followers. His dedication, commitment and loyalty to Celtic since he was captured as a 13-year-old "S" form signing epitomises in every way the real meaning of wanting to play and win for Celtic. Since his first appearance for Celtic in a League Cup match against Stenhousemuir in 1975, followed by his full first-team baptism at Pittodrie against Aberdeen not many weeks later, Roy has been a player who has never given less than his absolute best.

Having won League Championship, Scottish Cup and League Cup medals with the club, international honours and also the captaincy of the Scotland team, Roy could be forgiven for starting to think that he has achieved all the honours any top footballer could hope to win. However, I know he has an abiding ambition to win a European honour with Celtic and with his spirit and determination, who would bet against him achieving that goal?

Since he is still only 28 years old, despite 12 years at the top in football, I'm certain he will scale many heights before he hangs up his boots sometime in the future. In the meantime I have pleasure in commending his story to date, as contained in the pages of this book.

John McGinn,
Chairman,
Celtic Football Club.

Introduction

THURSDAY, 28 May, 1987, will go into Celtic folklore. It was the day Billy McNeill returned to Parkhead as manager for the second time, around 20 years almost to the day after the club's most famous victory in the European Cup final against Inter Milan.

Chairman Jack McGinn described it as "the return of the prodigal son". I first heard the momentous news on television after I returned from a coaching session at Butlin's Holiday Camp in Ayr. The Press had been told an hour before. To say I was stunned was to put it mildly. I had no hint of such a drastic change in the club set-up.

Davie Hay was as shocked as me. I was told later he met Neil Mochan as he went through the main door at Parkhead for an appointment with the chairman and made a joke that he must have been called in because a much on-off Australian tour had been put back on again. However, the reason for his summons was nothing so simple and gave him no reason to laugh. He was about to be told his four-year reign as the manager was over.

The decision of the directors took everyone in the dressing-room by surprise. Davie had told us in the clearest language that he would be around this season and actually told us his approach would be much harder and that discipline would be sharpened. He wasn't given the chance to implement this even though he had bought Mick

McCarthy from Manchester City for £500,000 and seemed to be preparing for another season. Licence to spend this kind of money — a record for our club — seemed to confirm this. However, we must face the fact that the "lift" of Big Billy returning was something the club needed badly, however sympathetic we may all have felt for the departing boss. Billy's enthusiasm immediately began to rub off on everyone. The place bubbled like a volcano about to erupt. We felt confident again. If the leadership was to change, Billy was the only man for the job. The names of Kenny Dalglish and Lou Macari had been mentioned as possibles but I always thought if there was to be any movement Billy McNeill was the only candidate.

He was hardly in the door when he held a players' meeting and set out his brand of law and order. We were told, for instance, that we mustn't wear jeans. The manager said he had no doubt there were smart jeans and sloppy jeans but he couldn't tell the difference. He wanted us to look smart on all occasions. Billy McNeill is not the kind of person who encourages arguments about his orders. No one attempted to do so.

He went on to tell us that Rangers had thrown down a gauntlet and it was up to us to pick it up and fight to win. High standards had been set at Ibrox and we had to improve on them. Nobody pretended this would be easy but it is the kind of challenge Celtic have loved over the years. The players didn't need to be told that Rangers winning the title for the first time in nine years had put pressure on us. They had to spend around £2½ million to overtake Celtic who have been a good deal more successful than them in the last 20 years.

Rangers have been chasing us quite a lot but they bought big and wisely to change the situation. In our view it is only temporary. We've now got to outmatch them again. It will not be easy because they are very professional. Having said this, there was little between us last season — a victory for them against us in the Skol Cup, when even Rangers admitted we were better, and separated by six points in the Premier League. Billy McNeill will not spend, spend, spend, as Graeme Souness has been able to do. He will get there on a much tighter budget.

Ignore the fact that Billy's record in England wasn't all that good. Aston Villa are in the Second Division but they were headed there when he took over. His previous club, Manchester City, also went down but their manager, Jimmy Frizzell, made it clear that was his responsibility. I feel Billy didn't have the finance at either club. Both

Together again . . . Billy McNeill and Roy Aitken in smiling mood at Parkhead.

had squandered cash before he got there. He had no room in which to manoeuvre. For instance, when he sold Steve Hodge to Spurs for £750,000, he got only £200,000 of this to buy a replacement even though the club was in a perilous position in the First Division. What I know — all of us do — is that in his previous five years as manager Billy won three championships and the Scottish Cup and League Cup. That's some record.

Billy is a Celtic man and this didn't change even after he left for Maine Road and then Villa Park. He was always associated with Celtic and when he returned to comment for television on a couple of our cup finals I detected a bias in our favour.

Does that really surprise you? This is the man we all called "Caesar" when he held the European Cup aloft in Lisbon — the first British skipper to do so — after Celts had beaten the great Inter Milan 2-1. He was one of the most successful players in Scottish football history but it was predominantly in a Celtic jersey.

He cost Celtic the princely sum of £250 when he was bought from Blantyre Victoria. Has there ever been a better football investment? He played 831 matches for the club and 29 times for Scotland, as well as nine Scottish League and five under-21 appearances. It surprised nobody, except maybe Billy himself, when he was awarded the MBE in the 1974 birthday honours list. As a player he led Celtic to nine championships in a row from 1966 and captained seven Scottish Cup-winning teams as well as appearing in another five finals on the losing side and skippering seven League Cup triumphs. He also lost in two other League Cup finals.

This is the man who has come back to lead Celtic. His record is second to none, so good that Celtic realised they couldn't do without him any longer. I can think of no greater compliment to a person so deeply involved in Celtic affairs over 30 years. Paradise was lost to him only temporarily.

Last season was only my third in 12 years without a competitive trophy . . . one under Jock Stein and two with Davie Hay. Our morale was low. Winning becomes a habit and it's very hard to accept an empty trophy cabinet. We needed a good perk up and that's what the change of management has given us. We had slackened off in the little things, like punctuality for training. That has now stopped. We have to be ready to train by 9.05 every morning. Punctuality is now nearly as important as scoring goals and maybe the two are related. Players guilty of silly dissension on the pitch are fined because their absence from the team on accumulated points is so vital.

One thing Celtic have been lacking for some time is an out-and-out stopper-style centre-back. In fact, a defender in the mould of the manager himself. I'm not saying that Mick McCarthy is identical to Big Billy but the job he does is similar. Mick will be a good signing for us. Young Paul McGugan had done well but, in the long run, he may profit from McCarthy's signing. He will now be given more time to gain experience.

Celtic's defence has taken a lot of stick but I think much of it has been unfair. We are the type of side who play with flair and throw men forward — maybe more often than we should. It is a gamble but we are prepared to take chances in the interests of entertainment. Mick is hard and uncompromising. He has already demonstrated his worth. Oddly, he was signed for Manchester City by Billy McNeill. The price from Barnsley was £200,000, so here is another example of our manager's ability to spot talent and make a tidy profit for a club. Billy told me he had no idea when Mick signed for Celtic that he would be joining him. I have not the slightest reason to doubt this.

Bobby Lennox puts a matey armlock on Brian McClair.

Anyway, it was our double good fortune. Billy was the first to spot the talents of Steve Archibald, Gordon Strachan and Brian McClair.

Their current transfer values are many times the price Billy paid for them at Aberdeen and Celtic.

The ability to assess talent is vital in a manager. He must be able to visualise a boy's ability in manhood in the style of a clairvoyant. Charlie Nicholas and Paul McStay emerged from the scouting system initiated by Billy in his first Parkhead management venture.

Losing Brian McClair and Mo Johnston has been a tremendous blow. It makes it an uphill fight for us in the League. They could be expected to score around 70 goals between them in a season. So their departure leaves a considerable gap and especially in a team who rely on bold attacking play more than most. However, I feel that if our fans are that wee bit patient they will get the results they so desperately want. I am sure of that.

This season we will be playing in the UEFA Cup. We were jealous, but not nastily, of Dundee United and thought them thoroughly unlucky to lose in the final to Gothenburg. Celtic will always give praise where it is due and that was true last season of Tannadice. It was a great feat to go as far as they did in the UEFA competition, beating Barcelona and Borussia Munchengladbach on the way.

I feel deeply about the fact that in my spell at Parkhead we haven't managed to get past the quarter-finals in Europe. I'm desperate to be in a final and winning. This said, you will realise how much I envied Davie Narey. United's luck ran out in the two-legged final. They had some good fortune, especially in Barcelona and Munchengladbach, but against Gothenburg they first of all had to perform on a terrible pitch in Sweden and at home didn't rise to their usual heights. Like United, Gothenburg were a good all-round team. Their styles were similar. Jim McLean was generous in the things he said about the winners afterwards. I believe the fans respect this kind of sportsmanship.

I wasn't surprised when Jim was selected as manager of the year by the media. What a disappointment it must have been for him to lose out in the League, Scottish Cup final and then the UEFA competition. Jim was not taken in by the argument that it was splendid to be in the running in all three competitions. He said wryly that he would rather have won one and missed out altogether in the other two. I always got along well with the United boss when he was Scotland's assistant manager. And despite the image he portrays he has a good sense of humour. Yes, he laughs a lot.

Billy McNeill, however, has always been my No. 1. I was devastated when he left. We get on well but, more important for me, I have had most success under him. Next best is Alex Ferguson, who I thought was tremendous during the World Cup in Mexico.

Having said these nice things about the north-east I must add that United and Aberdeen have had their fling at the top. The Old Firm are about to take over again. Celtic and Rangers will be back as the dominant twosome of Scottish football. The take-over is in process. I feel this is a good thing for the game. There is the altruistic opinion that honours should go round. But how many clubs take 10,000 and more fans to all away games?

Hearts have the next biggest away following, but smaller clubs certainly get a cash spin-off from a successful Old Firm. You may argue that football is about sport and so it is. It also concerns survival and to do this clubs must have people flocking through the turnstiles.

Parkhead fairly bustled last season and so did Ibrox. None could have forecast a return to such healthy crowds. And this is why I say winning Celtic and Rangers sides will be good — once again — for football. I don't expect Hearts or Hibs, Dundee United or Aberdeen to rush in shouting agreement. Their annual club balance sheets may do it for them.

It will be up to the other teams to knock us off our pedestals. Yes, I think Celtic will be back up on one very shortly, inspired by good management. Our biggest problem will be consolidating after losing such important players in the summer. Big Billy will give us that extra push to send us back to the top.

There has been speculation about how the Celtic club should be designed in the future. It is appropriate to raise this going into the club's centenary year. Should we go public as Rangers did nearly 60 years ago? The directors say, "No". It will continue as a private limited company and they will continue to control Celtic's destiny going into the 21st century. It is an important job for, at the end of the day, the Board are really answerable to the fans. It is their club. The subject has obviously been carefully examined and I am sure what has been decided is right.

Maintaining clubs at the highest level calls for considerable financial skills. Sponsorship money is now an important factor. CR Smith, the double glazing company, are putting at least £750,000 into the club over the next three years. They will benefit, so will

Celtic and, most important of all, so will the spectators with steadily improving facilities because of this kind of involvement. No one will be a loser. And that's the kind of deal I like for Celtic, on and off the pitch.

8 August 1987: Andy Walker scores in Celtic's opening game against Morton. Davie Wyllie is the diving keeper.

Chapter 1

WALKING TO PARADISE

IT was a typically chill but dry October night in 1972 when I stepped off the Ardrossan train at the Central Station in Glasgow literally to walk to Paradise. In that month the Queen and the Duke of Edinburgh celebrated their silver wedding and Alex Ferguson, then a player with Falkirk, led a successful Players' Union revolt against the SFA system of administering discipline.

None of the other travellers hurrying about their business had the slightest idea who I was, since Robert Sime Aitken was at the time barely 14. My main claim to fame was playing football for St Andrew's Academy at Saltcoats on Saturday mornings and Ayr United Boys' Club in the afternoons.

My dad didn't know Glasgow well which was why we had left the family Hillman Hunter at home. I had a good look around the station to get my bearings as I had been in the big city only on a few occasions myself for shopping. Off we set, not by taxi or bus but on the feet I never really thought — despite all my dreams — would sweep me to the captaincy of Celtic and Scotland.

As we trudged along Argyle Street, past Glasgow Cross and on to London Road it didn't seem much of a distance at all. In fact, in my frame of mind, it seemed a nice leisurely walk. If there had been snow drifts it would have been the same. You see, I was on my way to sign an "S" form for Celtic and would be paid the princely sum of £5 a week, which really didn't even cover my expenses for kit and travel.

Sean Fallon met me and my dad — his name is John, by the way, and he works as a crane-driver at Ardrossan Harbour — at the front door and in no time I had signed the paper which set me off on my way to football stardom.

Stardom? I never quite see myself as a star. I am a player first and foremost. A supporter of Celtic — and, of course, Scotland — with the joint aims of helping the team to win and pleasing the fans. I have heard it said that today's footballers and the people who pay them are a distance apart. This has never seemed to be a fact to me or my team-mates. When I hear the affectionate shouting of the fans — "Feed the Bear!" — I feel sometimes as if they're at my side. And that's the way it should be. They're in my team too!

I enjoy being called "The Bear". It's a welcome change from "Shirley" which is my nickname among the other players because I had long curly hair as a boy. But a "Bear" I most certainly am not as a person. And I don't eat raw meat before I go on to the pitch. In fact, I am a happily married family man. My wife is Jane and children Ashley and John and we live in much the same style as the average family. What luxuries we have are all thanks to football, of course. Even though I took seven 'O' levels I lost momentum in my studies because I was progressing rather more quickly at Parkhead than I had expected.

In fact, I very nearly signed for Ayr United. Ally MacLeod, then on his first stint as Ayr United manager a few years before bossing Scotland in Argentina, wanted to sign me. I was playing for Ayr United Boys' Club at the time. Ally said he liked me but at the same time Ayr had their quota of "S" form players. "Would I wait awhile?" Some people told me I'd be better at Somerset Park than Parkhead — even if I were given the chance — as there might be only half a dozen boys at Ayr against maybe 20 with Celtic. It was all a question of opportunity.

It so happened the father of one of my teachers at St Andrew's — Michael Murray — was Celtic's scout in Ayrshire and, unknown to me, he had been watching me for a couple of years. Within a couple of weeks of Ally talking to my dad, John Murray was at my door offering an "S" form signing for Celtic.

I was just a month off my 14th birthday. "Would I sign?" seemed the daftest question in the world. How could anybody stop me

Still only a schoolboy but Roy looks the part of a future star.

signing for the club I supported but had never at that point actually seen in the flesh. I had had no time to go to Parkhead to watch them. Saturday meant playing in the morning for my school, being picked up by dad and driven to the Ayr BC match. So there wasn't too much time for spectating.

Ayr United, of course, weren't pleased about me signing for Celtic but my ambition was high and I took the view that if you're going to do anything it should be with the best.

At first Celtic didn't insist on me changing anything. It was a good set-up with the Ayr BC and I was happy, so they said I should carry on. Eventually, of course, I began training once a week at Parkhead and then finally John Higgins, the Celtic chief scout at the time, told me it would be better if I joined Celtic Boys' Club as I would be seen there by Jock Stein himself. Frank Cairney, the general manager of the Boys' Club team, made me captain right away. By this time, incidentally, I had played against England, Ireland, and Wales at under-15 schoolboy level, with Jim Melrose and Davie Dodds in the same side.

Roy Aitken dressed smartly for impending stardom in his St Andrew's Academy rig-out.

I played only a year for Celtic BC but it was a memorable 12 months. At the end of it I was named Player of the Year. Alan Brazil was in the same team, though he never signed for Celtic and John McCluskey, George's brother, was the best youngster I played with. Sadly, he was knocked out of the game because of injury while still only a Celtic reserve. He had great potential. I remember in practice matches he was fantastic. He was an outside-left and Danny McGrain would usually be in against him. Danny would be heard frequently complaining, "Oh, not John McCluskey again!" The fact that John's career ended so quickly because of a bad knock illustrates just how insecure a footballer's life can be.

When I was still 16 I had to make a big decision. I had taken seven 'O' levels and planned to sit my Highers the next year. I was told Celtic wanted to call me up immediately. So in 1975, while still at school, I signed provisionally. I was paid £25 a week and that was good money. I then had to train twice a week and, on a Friday morning, I would telephone Parkhead and John Clark would tell me what I had to do on the Saturday.

My first reserve game was at Pittodrie. I shared the centre-half role with George Connelly and we lost 4-1. What a hammering! When I was still 16, and after only a couple of months in the reserves, I was chosen in the League Cup pool to play Stenhousemuir. I was on the bench watching players like Kenny Dalglish, Bobby Lennox, Danny McGrain, Andy Lynch, Roddie MacDonald, Pat McCluskey and Paul Wilson. Ten minutes from the end Roddie was taken off and I replaced him. That gave me the feel of the first team. Two weeks later, on 24 September 1975, to be precise, in the return, I played the full game at right-back — and the winger against me was a flier!

At school the lads didn't treat me in any special way. I was training at Parkhead twice weekly and preparing for Highers in English, Maths, History and Biology. I lost interest a wee bit and wasn't studying as hard as I should have been because of the way things were going for me with Celtic. There was, however, one major difference at school. The headmaster, Mr Tom Finn, was a Celtic fan. If he saw me in the school library he would ask me to his room, pour a cup of tea and talk about how I was playing. I remember him reading from the *Daily Record* and looking up laughingly to say: "You're getting a good write-up here, Roy."

In February 1976 I played alongside Johannes Edvaldsson in my

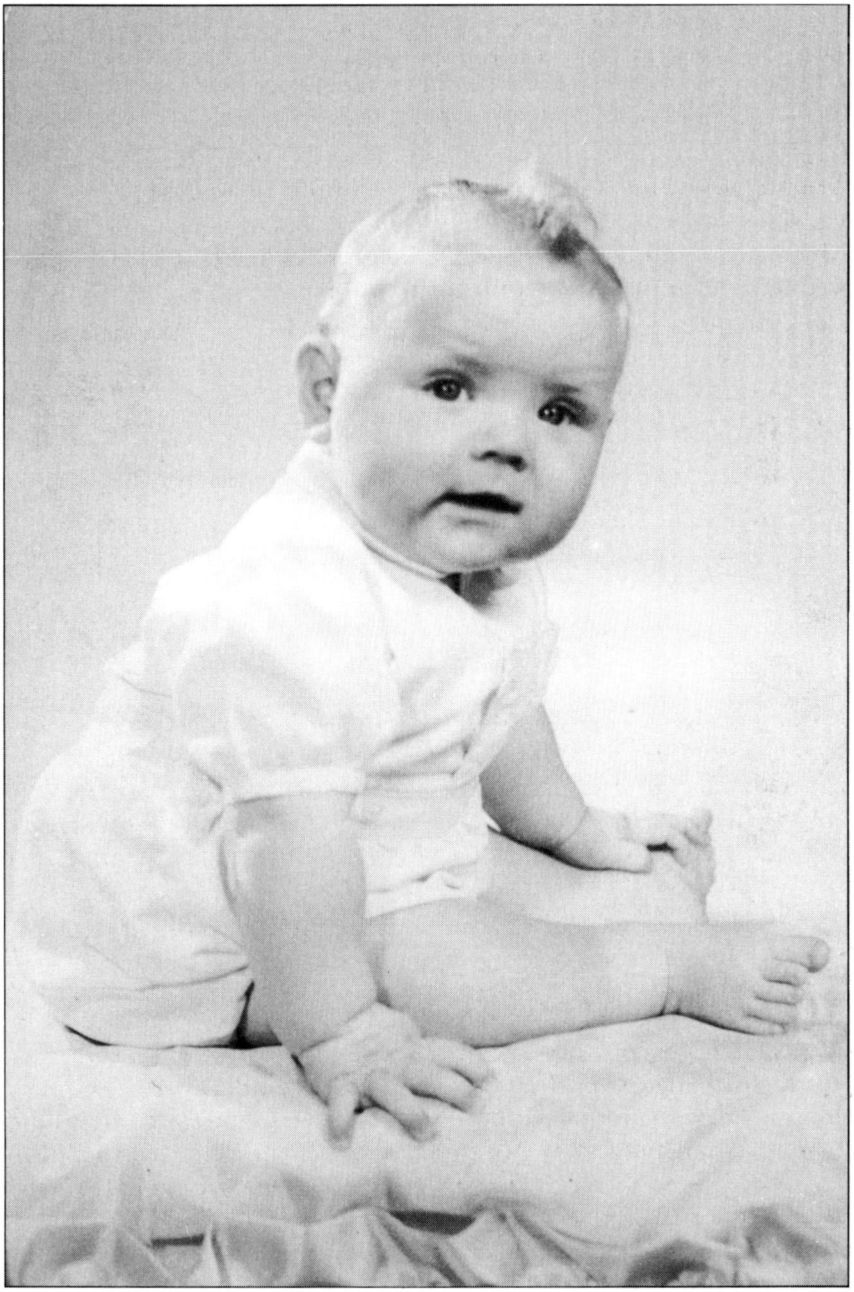

Oops . . . "Why is everybody looking at me?".

first Premier League game, against Aberdeen, and we won 1-0. Bobby Lennox played centre-forward that night and scored in the last couple of minutes. Pittodrie, by the way, is still one of my favourite grounds.

I passed my Highers in English and Maths and played right through to the end of the season in the first team. The long climb to the top had begun. I also began to realise how much I owed to my dad John and my mum Lily. They clearly had made many sacrifices to help me in my career. This book allows me the opportunity of saying a special "thank you" to them for being right behind me from the very beginning.

Chapter 2

MY STEIN ERA

CELTIC, remarkably, have had only six managers since the club was established in 1888; Willie Maley, Jimmy McStay, Jimmy McGrory, Jock Stein, Billy McNeill, Davie Hay and McNeill again. By far the most famous and successful was Jock Stein, who led Celtic to world record nine championships and won everything else in the history of the game, including being the first British manager to take the European Cup back to Britain.

When I first got to know Mr Stein he was still recovering from the effects of a bad car accident which happened on the dual carriageway from Carlisle to Glasgow while he had been returning from a holiday. I remember my pal Bobby Lennox telling me at the time that the boss had mellowed a bit when he came back to work. He now had Davie McParland as his assistant and I had the impression they didn't get on too well although there was never any serious evidence of this.

However, I already knew all about Stein the Disciplinarian, Stein the Tactician and Master of all he Surveyed. At the very height of his career he had run everything at Parkhead including the number of complimentary tickets which had to be checked at the front door by Bill Peacock. So, having been told all this, Big Jock was something of a god to me. Since I was only a boy I couldn't relate to him well enough to have a long conversation, but I quickly found out that he knew everything that had been going on even when he was lying in a hospital bed seriously ill.

I had played about a dozen games in season 1975-76 and before the start of the new season Mr Stein got us all together to talk about what was ahead. Davie McParland was with him. The boss took me to one side and chatted about my game. He told me he didn't think I was yet strong enough physically to play an out and out centre-half. He told me he would be bringing in Roddie MacDonald, but would find a place for me.

In fact, I missed the first two games and then I was chosen for midfield, positioning myself — on instructions, of course — just in front of the back four. This worked out splendidly for me and was the start of a personal respect I always felt for the Great Man.

There was so much admiration for him in football it was incredible. There was an aura about him and when he walked into a room everyone stopped talking and waited for him to speak. Friends tell me that before games he used to rub his face until it was red and would then storm into the dressing-room affecting the idea he was furious. And that was before the game kicked off. He was "Mr Celtic".

My first very clear example of his tactical know-how was at the end of season 1976-77 when we had won the League and Scottish Cup double and just missed the League Cup as well by losing 2-1 to Aberdeen because of an extra-time goal by Davie Robb. That was one the best teams I played in, by the way. Kenny Dalglish was in the side and so were Pat Stanton, Danny McGrain, Ronnie Glavin and John Doyle who was later to die so tragically in an accident in his home.

In the close season we played in Australia and Singapore against Red Star of Belgrade. They murdered us 4-1 in a Thursday game prior to us playing them again on the Sunday. We had opted for our usual cavalier attacking type game which was right up the street of a clever side like Red Star who defended brilliantly and hit on the break. Big Jock then got us together and changed our style completely. Imagine Celtic playing defensively. Well, we did. "Leave them with the ball," we were told. "Be defensive and hit them on the break and we'll see how they like their own brand of football being thrown back at them."

In the first game the Yugoslavs had run around as though we

The long curly hair which earned Roy the nickname "Shirley".

weren't there with our orthodox 4-3-3 go-everywhere style. Our new approach changed all that. I had never played like this. We went back and sat in our own half. We drew 1-1 with them and then subsequently beat them 2-0. That was my first personal experience of the Midas touch of a truly great manager. He spotted what should have been obvious and told us how to rectify our mistakes. That to me is quality management.

Jock Stein's record will be in football folklore for the rest of time, so it was something of an honour for my career to be fashioned at the start by such a man. Other young players envied those of us who were lucky enough to be at Parkhead then.

Although Davie McParland took the training at that time, Mr Stein was usually around and that big left hand used to shoot out as he bawled from the side. There was no let up, no slacking in training when he was there. He made certain everybody worked as they were expected to do to the last kick of every match. He pushed us through training. And this was him mellowing!

Bertie Auld told us that Jock had all kinds of ways of finding out what players were doing. On a Monday morning he would walk into the dressing-room and ask: "Wasn't Sinatra great on BBC last night?" Sure as anything somebody would agree and Jock would pounce. "He wasn't on the telly . . . where were you when you should have been in bed?"

Jimmy Johnstone — what a marvellous player he was and how popular he still is with the fans — was once sitting in a bar having a quiet shandy when the phone went and Jock Stein asked to speak to him. Wee Jimmy couldn't believe it. "The boss's spies are everywhere," he said. In fact, some well-meaning fan had phoned the park and spoken to Mr Stein, so he thought he would demonstrate to Wee Jinky how difficult it was to do anything without him knowing. Nevertheless big Jock loved to talk about Jimmy years later. He clearly had a great admiration for the Wee Man.

The boss was strict even on items like food. I remember being at Aberdeen for a game and we sat down for our usual plate of soup with a main course, usually steak or chicken. We were allowed one glass of milk but no sweet. And there were no luxuries like Cokes with our meals. I remember we set Joe Craig up by telling him to have a prawn cocktail. Sure enough, the waiter had hardly put it on the table when Jock Stein appeared and roared at Joe, "You wouldn't have prawn cocktail if you were at home on a Friday night,

The happy look of a Cup final winner.

would you?" Big Joe said that was true. The prawn cocktail was shipped away and Joe got his soup like the rest of us.

Another time I recall being in Inverness sitting with Andy Lynch, Bobby Lennox and Peter Latchford. Jock Stein always took a seat where he could see everything, working along the same theory as a gunslinger in the Wild West, never sitting with his back to the door. He always made sure he had a clear view of everything that was happening. He was very much in my line of vision and I remember forgetting myself and calling on the waiter: "Could I please have a glass of . . . water?" I had been going to say "milk" but big Jock knew I had already had my one-glass ration so I had the presence of mind to change my request at the last minute. Mr Stein gave me the hint of a smile which he reserved for a nearly bad boy.

Despite all the football action he had taken part in, Mr Stein was nervous before big occasions. Success meant so much to him as well as to us. And he wanted Celtic to win so desperately. I was only with him for two cup finals, when the Dons beat us in that extra-time game and then when Andy Lynch gave us victory over Rangers from a penalty in the same season, 1976-77. I will always remember him putting his arm around my shoulder after we had lost to Aberdeen and saying I had played well and Celtic were unlucky not to win. This was a demonstration of compassion. He realised, as part of his instinct as a great manager, that it was my first final and I would be really disappointed. Disappointed? I was shattered.

When I came under Mr Stein's discipline with Scotland he had changed again. His authority, although still very much there, was not as tight. For instance, he didn't clamp down as heavily at meal times. I think he felt he had the cream of the players around him and each individual should know exactly at that stage how to look after himself. It wasn't his job to lay down the law as it was at a club. I also felt I could speak to him a lot more easily. He was more relaxed and there was more fun about him.

At pre-game talks he went into details of the opposition much more thoroughly. At club level he worried more about how we played as Celtic players than about the opposition whom most of us knew well in any event. Scotland players, though, were given very explicit details about the opposition, how good or bad in the air they were, and a particular player's pace and strong or weak foot. And even about their attitude.

Jock Stein's death and everything leading up to the awful moment

On the ball for Scotland.

when we were given the desperately sad news remains etched in my memory. All week he had looked unwell. I couldn't work it out because although there was tremendous pressure over qualifying for Mexico, as always, he seemed able to handle this as a person. In the few days before our match with Wales at Cardiff he was drawn and really let the match look after itself. Of course, he had Alex Ferguson with him and there was no doubt Fergie took a lot of the weight off his shoulders.

Before the Wales match we had played England and Iceland and I remember Jock Stein changed the Wembley tactics dramatically because of a single change in Bobby Robson's side. I was to have been a defensive marker with Alex McLeish and Willie Miller was to be the spare man. On the morning of the game, however, I was told everything was altered and that we would line up 4-3-3 with me in the middle to challenge Bryan Robson. It worked well. Richard Gough scored the winner and Mr Stein said I had a good game.

We had beaten Iceland 1-0 thanks to a late Jim Bett goal and we weren't without luck, I'll tell you. So the Cardiff match was vital. We needed a draw at least. As the history books record Davie Cooper made sure of it with a penalty goal.

In those last few minutes, we knew we were going to qualify for the World Cup play-off and for the second time in eight years it was amidst controversy and against Wales. But we also knew that Jock Stein had been taken into the dressing-room area unwell, though at that time we were unaware of the seriousness.

In the dressing-room we should have been in a celebratory mood at the end of the match. Scotland had made it to Mexico. But there was near silence as we changed and waited for more news. It must have been 20 minutes later that we were told. I looked at physio Jim Steel's face and knew without any words that the worst had happened. "Steely" and big Jock had been great friends for many years, so, naturally, he took the news very badly.

The entire Scottish squad went from a high to utter dejection in the space of a few minutes. On the plane home, no one referred to the game. We were either silent or recalled the great things about the Stein legend.

It was the end of the dynasty of a man who in a lifetime worked his way from the very bowels of the earth as a pit-worker to one of the top places in world sport. Bill Shankly said of him after Celtic won the European Cup in 1967, "John, you're immortal". This was, of course, one of Shankly's extravagant but pardonable exaggerations. In truth, Jock Stein, CBE, came as close to being immortal as any human can.

His era has come and gone, but his deeds and the legend which accompanied them will be remembered for ever. Under his management Celtic won 25 major trophies which is, by any standard, phenomenal. This was the array of honours which Jock Stein inspired: The European Cup; Scottish League Championship ten times (including nine in a row to equal the world record of MTK Budapest of Hungary and CDNA Sofia of Bulgaria); the Scottish Cup eight times; and the League Cup on six occasions. Celtic's full record during the wonderful Jock Stein reign was: played 421, won 296, drawn 66, lost 59. They scored 1,111 goals and conceded only 413. In season 1973-74 when Celtic won the title for the ninth time they lost only four matches out of the 34 played to total 53 points — four ahead of Hibs. I doubt very much if this truly magnificent record will ever be surpassed.

Chapter 3

HOW METHODS CONTRAST

IT is interesting to compare the techniques of managers, and with Jock Stein as an example, examine my two other Parkhead bosses, Billy McNeill and Davie Hay. This reveals contrasting methods. Of the three, Billy has always spoken most about opposing players.

When he first came back to Parkhead from Aberdeen in June 1978, he took me to one side and said that although he would always be one of the boys he was now also the manager and at times everyone would have to bear this in mind. I felt in little doubt that this included me. In fact, no one is ever in any doubt about where he stands with him. He is a plain and frank speaker. In his early days as manager everything that happened at the park involved big Billy in some way. Nothing has changed. It is still his style. He takes the training and plays in the practice games.

Billy steered Celtic cleverly through a transitional period at the end of the Stein era. He signed Murdo McLeod and Davie Provan and brought in John Kelman as chief scout to get the youth policy cracking. He will always do well. He's that type of person. This was best illustrated after Aston Villa sacked him. Within a few days he had offers from Airdrie and then Kuwait and others were in the pipeline if Celtic had not moved so decisively.

The situation now facing the manager at the start of his second

Roy jumps above everyone but his header against Aberdeen is played out by 'keeper Jim Leighton.

time around is once again a period of transition with the playing staff weakened by departures and particularly in the important striking area.

I get on splendidly with Billy — probably because I have so much respect for him — but he can be ruthless with players when he feels it is required. Discipline is an important part of his code. Players must work to rule.

The most obvious thing about Davie Hay is that he is a nice man. Nobody could ask for a fairer person but, sadly, manners are sometimes mistaken for weakness.

Davie was the "quiet man" in his dealing with us. Whereas Billy is a very good after-dinner speaker and media interviewee, Davie was a target for the teasing satire of the radio programme *Naked Radio*. Typical of him, though, he laughed as loudly as anybody about it. He wasn't in the slightest put out.

I have had more success under our present manager and naturally this inclines me in his favour. Under his direction we won three championships, the Scottish Cup and the League Cup. I am positive that this kind of success will be repeated.

His knowledge of opponents is exceptional. If we played Aberdeen two Saturdays running he would still have something new and interesting to tell us about them. Billy lectures us about not turning our backs at throw-ins or free kicks. He spotlights, for instance, that Aberdeen take frees quickly and we should get a man in front of the ball sharply. He repeats these little things and they add up to something important by the end of his talk. Nothing is left to chance. If anything goes wrong we can usually look back and say the point was covered in the pre-game discussion.

Billy has charisma. He has done everything as a player, including captaining the European Cup winners in Lisbon on that great night in 1967. His form on the pitch was really something. So if there is a swagger about him then that's the way it should be. It is his entitlement.

Management is what Billy is best at nowadays. He does it well, as we are seeing for a second time at Parkhead. Players meeting him for the first time must get to know him. He has to be approached at the right time. Choose the wrong moment and you pay the price.

In his first managerial spell with us Billy got the best out of players like Davie Provan, Frank McGarvey, and Charlie Nicholas. He is repeating this now except that some of the names are different. I remember — like Jock Stein — Billy could tell Charlie exactly what he had been doing over the weekend. And woe betide him if it was something of which the manager disapproved. Billy admires guys like Charlie, although not all players get on quite so well with him. He comes into the dressing-room more often than Jock Stein did in my time, or Davie Hay, for that matter. Billy wants to be in on everything that is happening. For example, if he sees a player rushing away from training he wants to know where he is headed and why. He jokes and laughs with us. He always digs Bobby Lennox and myself up about the fact that we are perhaps reluctant to part

Poolside with Charlie Nicholas and Mo Johnston.

with our money unless we have to. "You Ayrshire mob are all the same," he jokes. At least, I think he is joking!

We were all a bit bewildered when Billy left Parkhead the first time. His partnership with John Clark was broken up suddenly in the close season with Billy going to Manchester City. Now he is back and nothing seems to have changed about him. He is larger than life.

One of the key factors about Stein, McNeill and Hay is that they are, or were, very Celtic-minded, having played key roles themselves on the pitch in green and white jerseys. Billy still remembers his playing days, as was very clearly instanced when the Lisbon Lions got together again 20 years on. But Davie is a player's man as well and I hope he will pop up again soon as manager of another club. Davie's philosophy is that if a player does his job on the park he is entitled to lead his own style of life away from it. I am not sure that our present boss entirely agrees with this. Certainly there was always respect and liking for Hay. The two qualities don't always go hand in hand. He clamped down once or twice on Mo Johnston but so long as he was scoring and doing his work for the team he wasn't too critical in other ways. Davie made sure that Mo was training hard and generally approaching his work properly at the park. For a manager Davie was very laid back. But he became more involved with us after Frank Connor, then assistant manager, left and later joined Raith Rovers. The players preferred him to be part of the training because, at the end of the day, it is the manager who has to take the stick if things go wrong.

Davie steered us to a Scottish Cup win and to the Championship. Okay, we won the title on the last Saturday of season 1985-86 when Hearts lost 2-0 at Dens Park while we were hammering St Mirren 5-0 and it has been said that we were lucky. I don't think so. We took 16 points out of our last eight games and put tremendous pressure on Hearts who finally couldn't handle it. In fact, we were unbeaten in our last 16 League encounters. We kept plugging away — as Davie Hay said we should — and hoped Hearts would slip up. We thought that something would happen and it did . . . apart from us scoring 21 goals in the last eight matches.

In February, we welcomed Tommy Craig as first-team coach. He played with Aberdeen, Sheffield Wednesday, Newcastle United, Aston Villa, Swansea, Carlisle and Hibs, so he knows the game. He was also assistant manager of Hibs before Alex Miller moved to Easter Road from Love Street. However, Hay remained involved in the

CR SMITH

training side until the big change was made. We are happy that Tommy is now in the McNeill mould and is toiling away happily. The manager clearly rates his coaching work.

What different endings seasons can have. When we won the title so dramatically from Hearts we had a cavalier attitude against St Mirren and were leading 4-0 at half-time. Mo Johnston scored a couple and the second was surely the goal of the season. Brian McClair also scored and Paul McStay grabbed the fourth. When Mo got his fantastic second and our third of the match we made six passes without a Saints man touching the ball and then McClair released it perfectly for Johnston to score.

The news wobbled Hearts. I know for a fact that they came out at half-time and said to some of the Dundee lads: "Celtic are four in front at Paisley . . . that doesn't look good for us." So in the end Hearts couldn't live with the leadership and they lost 2-0 with both goals scored by Dundee's Albert Kidd.

We knew seven minutes from the end at Love Street that the title was ours. A tremendous roar went up when the fans heard on their radios that Dundee had scored and it was even louder four minutes later when Kidd got his second. To be fair, Hay had encouraged us to think the flag could still be ours although Hearts had been in front for so long. What a disappointment it must have been for Alex MacDonald and his players. But it underlined to them that Celtic are never beaten until the very final whistle.

Celtic fans ran on to the Paisley pitch at the end to salute a mighty achievement. Once I got up the tunnel, though, I was astonished to find Davie Hay in the dressing-room, calm as anything, smoking one of his favourite little cigars. I expected him to be doing his nut but he seemed to regard it all as routine. He didn't really, but that was the impression he gave.

Winning the title is a great achievement for a manager as well as the team so I couldn't help admiring his powers of restraint. He shook hands with us individually and said, "Well done." It was his typical low-key approach to most things. Of course, he was happy and there was a nice glint in his eyes. He could also be pleased about the fact that Celtic won the Reserve League Cup by beating Dundee 3-1 in the Dens Park final.

In the dug-out during matches Davie sat quietly and watched. There were a couple of exceptions but generally speaking his calmness was usual. This is the most striking difference between him

Everyone is happy because Celtic have just beaten Dundee United in the 100th Scottish Cup final.

and the exuberant McNeill. Davie applauded the other team as well and would say what a good pass an opponent made. Billy is more likely to inquire why they were allowed to make it. Billy plays each game in the dug-out. He didn't like losing as a player and this has continued into his management style. When Celtic lose, the idea of facing him in the dressing-room is a daunting prospect.

When we won the Scottish Cup with goals by Davie Provan and Frank McGarvey Davie Hay did lose his cool a bit and hugged each of us on the park. But that was his first major trophy victory and we had come back virtually from the dead to beat Dundee United 2-1.

I never heard Davie looking for credit. He believed that should go to the players and is really quite a modest family man. They say nice men never get on in football management. This is not entirely true. However, when last season ended in failure Davie had to pay the penalty. One explanation for his departure was that he was perhaps *too* nice.

Billy McNeill has an executive look about him. He dresses smartly and expects the players to do the same. He is rarely without a tie when not in a track suit. And when he walks into a crowded room there is no way he will be ignored. As he says, he can be one of the boys. But he can switch quickly to being a very tough boss. Bellshill is his home town and maybe it is significant that Sir Matt Busby comes from the same area. Sir Matt has been hugely successful at Old Trafford and has become a legend in his own lifetime. Our manager has the ability, the presence, and the management acumen to achieve similar status. Being the first Celtic manager in history to be invited to return to Paradise — and heading into our centenary year — seems to me to put him well on the way.

Chapter 4

'ADOPTED' BY CELTIC

EVERYTHING happened in a mad rush when I was in my last year at school. Celtic even had to "adopt" me so that I could play in a European tie in East Germany. The thing that thrilled me most was that I felt I was being groomed at Parkhead to fill the boots of Billy McNeill. It has turned out, of course, that I have been switched around as Billy never was.

Some things happened in an odd way. Sean Fallon had to telephone my school to make sure I could get away to travel with the first-team party going to Aberdeen. And although I was being marked down at first to do the No. 5 job it astounded me that I had been picked for Scotland under-15's and under-18's at midfield and full-back — but not as a centre-half. I was even chosen to captain the under-17 schoolboys for a big match in Greece. A basketball match! This clashed with my football preparations so I was forced to say no. It was very flattering all the same.

About that adoption. Celtic were drawn to meet Sachsenring Zwickau of East Germany in the European Cup Winners Cup quarter-final after good wins in earlier rounds against Valur of Iceland and Boavista of Portugal. This was at a stage in my career when I had appeared in only two Premier League games, against the Dons and Hibs. To my pleasant surprise, I was told I was to play. I went to school during the day and dashed to Seamill at nights for special European training.

This was my first experience of big-time European football. There was a crowd of 46,000 at Parkhead and I had a practical lesson in the art of stealing a valuable match-levelling goal. With just two minutes to go Celtic were leading by a single goal which Kenny Dalglish had scored five minutes from half-time. It would have put us in a reasonable position for the replay if only we could prevent them scoring. I was already thinking how enjoyable it would be, going behind the Iron Curtain for the first time with a goal lead for the second leg of the fixture.

Celtic were attacking furiously when the ball was suddenly cleared from the East German penalty area. I was standing at midfield with a gent called Ludwig Blank. There was nothing Blank about him, I can tell you. With a devastating burst of speed he gathered the ball and wheeled away from me. I was caught unawares and my lack of experience didn't help. Anyway, Herr Blank scored to make it 1-1. When I look back on the game I realise we had missed chances and in fact Bobby Lennox even failed from the penalty spot after Dalglish had been brought down.

Then came the special excitement for me. Because I was still only 17, permission for me to leave London had to be obtained from the Bow Street Magistrates Court. In effect they passed over my guardianship from my parents to Celtic FC. It was all very bewildering but I knew I was in safe hands, and would be handed back to my parents after the game.

Once through Checkpoint Charlie and into the East, Sean Fallon had to go to the police with the documents to show that I was an "adoptive child". I think even the German police saw the funny side of me having this kind of status and also being a footballer taking part in one of the most important European club football tournaments.

Just before the return match I had played in my first Old Firm game in front of 60,000, so my football education was well and truly under way. But we had no more luck at the Dimitroff Stadium than we had at Parkhead. We lost 1-0 to a goal scored by that man Blank again. It was a long-range "dipper".

However, we were all convinced that Celtic had scored a perfectly good goal three minutes from the end. Roddie MacDonald headed the ball in when we were making a final assault on the East German goal. It was disallowed, and I remember our dismay when the posturing Spanish referee ruled the effort out. The referee explained to the Press afterwards: "MacDonald pushed the German goalkeeper and for this reason I had no doubt it couldn't be a goal." Celtic had certainly dominated the game and didn't deserve to lose. It was a special disappointment for acting manager Sean Fallon. He would have loved to have gone home with the tonic of a victory for the recovering Jock Stein.

I learned a great deal from these two matches and not only about the style of Continental play. I found out that Europeans specialise in hanging back and hitting on the break. But, above all, I discovered that at this level successful teams can't afford to make mistakes. It is necessary to concentrate from the first kick to the last. A single error can mean disaster.

European football creates a great deal of interest for the fans but, having won the European Cup in 1967, we were always given special respect by our opponents. Nevertheless, in my time it has proved very difficult to get past the quarter-finals.

Chapter 5

MY LONGEST WALK

"NEVER mind the excuses . . . you're off!"

These six words will linger in my mind always. They were all that referee Bob Valentine said before showing me the red card in the Scottish Cup final against Aberdeen in May 1984. I became the first player to be dismissed from the final since Jock Buchanan, of Rangers, was sent off at Hampden in 1929. The despair, the indignity, the embarrassment, and my own personal torment were indescribable. Even now I have difficulty believing it actually happened.

I would have liked to give my interpretation of the incident at the time but this, of course, is not allowed. What I will do here for the first and only time is give my version of what happened and leave judgement to the reader.

The tackle involved Mark McGhee, now a team-mate at Parkhead. He lay on the ground for two minutes during the stoppage before I was given my marching orders. He then went on to grab the 2-1 winner for Aberdeen in extra-time and won the "Mr Superfit" award on the vote of reporters in the Hampden Press box. Mark is a good pal of mine now and all the boys joke with him about "taking a dive" in the final. But at the time many thought he had play-acted. It would be fair to say, of course, that no doubt others thought he had not.

However, let's go back to the 38th minute. McGhee went past Danny McGrain and Mark Reid. I was the last man. He came directly at me. He was in the inside-right position at the corner of the box. I had to come across him and, as he approached, he knocked the ball straight past me. I put my leg out and at the angle I body-checked and he went right over my leg.

In fact, I hardly touched him with the leg. It was my arm that caught him at the top of the hips. I actually hurt my arm. The effect spun me off my feet and I landed awkwardly. Mark went down in a heap and he lay there prostrate. He didn't move. I got up and Gordon Strachan, then with Aberdeen, was on the scene right away shouting to the referee that it was a bad tackle. Gordon is a guy I like. We get on well off the park. But on it he is a needler. He chats throughout a game and eventually can be very annoying. A good man to have on your side, mind you. But in opposition . . . oh, dear!

I looked round to see if McGhee was on his feet but he was still lying on the Hampden turf like a wounded war victim. Willie Miller appeared, too, for his pound of flesh. Willie seems to come up from a hole in the ground at these kind of incidents. Next I saw big Doug Rougvie running from Aberdeen's left-back position to our inside-right area. I told the lot of them to belt up and let the referee handle it.

McGhee wasn't hurt. I was sure of that. But I also knew the challenge could have looked worse than it was. It was a body check, not a vicious or malicious tackle.

Mr Valentine had booked me — I was one of eight to be yellow-carded — a minute from the end of the League Cup final a couple of months before when Rangers beat us 3-2 in extra-time and Ally McCoist got a hat-trick. Anyway, as 60,000 waited to find out what was to happen to me I tried to explain briefly that it was my arm more than anything which caused the Dons man to go down.

But the red card was up and I simply couldn't credit it. It was then that Mr Valentine uttered the fateful words, "Never mind the excuses . . . you're off!" He didn't even go through the formality of asking my name. He didn't need to. I had been in his black book several times before. As I began to jog to the pavilion I looked round and shouted to Strachan: "You didn't help me one little bit!" To be fair to Gordon, I think he was as surprised as me. I think he expected a booking and felt this would quieten me. Opponents know that a cautioned defender has to be careful. The yellow card is really a

A fine interception by Terry Butcher just ahead of Mark McGhee.

warning that one more mistake and the game ends for you.

Running off, hoping Hampden would open up and swallow me, I

thought about the overriding consideration in the judgement of a foul. This is intention. Hand on heart, all I intended to do was to get the ball.

In the dressing-room I sat stunned. I took my jersey off, threw my boots aside and just sat there wondering what on earth had happened. Jim Steele, our usually laughing physio, came in but stayed for only a minute. He quickly detected that I didn't want company. I had left Celtic's ten to battle. They were already a goal down and it didn't help that many considered Mark McGhee had elbowed Danny McGrain in the lead-up to the first goal before the ball went to Eric Black who just might have been offside as he scored.

At half-time my mates tried to console me. But flashing through my mind was the fact that we were second in the League and runners-up in the League Cup. We seemed to be going for the also-rans hat-trick. I spent the second half and the 30 minutes of extra-time sitting alone in a corner of the Directors' box. I didn't speak to a person.

It seemed that there were tackles which were worse than mine and which didn't lead to the same drastic punishment, but I accept that it is difficult for me to be objective. Friends told me they thought three other players committed fouls which looked worse than mine. This, of course, is a matter of opinion and is not a criticism of the referee whose judgements are the ones that count. Losing the Cup and being sent off was the worst combination of events which has ever happened to me in the game. But although I was in the depth of despair, quitting football never entered my mind. I'm not the type to run away.

At that time I was getting quite a few bookings, certainly more than now. People ask if I've altered my style but I haven't changed in any way. The possibility is that with experience and a place in Scotland's international team my stature in the game has gone up and I am regarded differently. Whatever has happened, I'm still the same but I'm not picking up as many bookings despite the SFA clamp-down.

When Paul McStay levelled the score in the 85th minute of that final, I was in seventh heaven, even though I realised in an instant if there was a replay I wouldn't be involved because of the automatic ban following an ordering off. I hoped the boys could hold out but in the extra-time it was just too much for them although the gallant ten played extremely well in the second half. My feeling was of having let

Roy's expression tells the story. . . Aberdeen have scored in the 1984 Cup final.

them down, leaving ten to fight on for so long in such a vital game. Thankfully the players didn't think this way.

Mark McGhee's winner in 98 minutes was all the more annoying because he wasn't a favourite of mine at that particular time! Afterwards, I didn't go up for my also-rans medal. Mark Reid collected it for me and handed it over in the dressing-room without ceremony.

My first after-match thoughts were for my wife, Jane. She was in the early stage of pregnancy before the birth of my son John and was in the Queen Mother Maternity Hospital in Glasgow for checks. She watched the game on a portable bedside TV. I knew how I felt and I was surprised how well she accepted my sending off. I was in a state and thought she might be as well. So it was a relief that she took it calmly.

I had promised to go to a supporters' club function at Coatbridge later in the evening. I decided there was only one thing I could do — go as I had promised. If we had won, I would have been there, so it was important to face the fans in defeat. The supporters were understanding and didn't talk a lot about the red card incident. They were all thoroughly disappointed about the defeat however.

If I hadn't faced the music then it's just possible I would have started asking myself if it was worth while continuing with football. I decided that holding my head up was the only way.

I pulled out of the Scotland squad to play England and France, feeling this was the practical thing to do. I telephoned Mr Stein and explained I felt it was better not to go, both because of my wife's state of health and what had happened in the final. Quite a few of the Aberdeen players were involved with Scotland — wee Gordon, Jim Leighton, Willie Miller, Mark McGhee and Alex McLeish — and I didn't want any friction. I'm not that type. But I thought it diplomatic to keep out of the way at that particular time. Mr Stein suggested I should still go to France, but I stuck to my guns. Anyway, I knew I could be useful to my wife around the house. I wanted to forget the season and start afresh.

McGhee scored with a header in the England match at Hampden Park and I was watching it on the telly. I gave him a cheer.

I was out of the Scots pool for a couple of seasons after that. Gordon moved to Manchester United and Mark went to Hamburg a few days after the final. So really the ordering off was never mentioned again — until Mark joined us at Parkhead. I get on well with him — as I do with my pal Gordon. That awful incident is forgotten unless we're having a joke. But when Mark appeared first of all the boys kept asking him: "Come on, Mark, show us you're version of that dive!" It was all banter, of course.

Mark still thinks it was a bad tackle although recently he brought a picture to Parkhead, given to him by a friend, which seemed to support my view that I caught him mainly with my arms. And the

Roy with his wife Jane and children John and Ashley.

lads joke about it often. Only the other day Tommy Burns shouted at a training session: "Hey, Roy, is Mark still saying you karate-chopped him?" It's a good laugh . . . now.

The fact that Mark played out 120 minutes and won the "Mr Superfit" award at least confirms that I didn't hurt him. People call me a "hard man". I resent that a bit. A "hard man" is somebody I associate with street fights but I'm definitely not that type. It's the last thing I would do. I'm a family man. I regard myself as a hard player. I'm a defender, so tackling is my business. But I do it fairly. The last thing I would want would be to injure an opponent. I've never been sent off or cautioned for retaliation or punching. My fouls are for honest challenges. Being a big bloke, the strength I put into tackles may sometimes look exaggerated. I'm not a win-at-any-cost type and, if I break the laws, it's because my natural enthusiasm has run away with me. That's the truth.

Billy McNeill was in the TV commentary box for that final and he explained afterwards: "I had just said on the air that Roy had no grounds for complaint when he was called over by Mr Valentine. He was due a booking. But I never expected him to be sent off. I don't think the tackle warranted that punishment. He made the decision to stop McGhee but I don't think there was any malicious intent." If Billy had thought otherwise, he would certainly have said so. He doesn't speak at any time with a forked tongue.

On the Monday after the final, McGhee flew to Hamburg and arranged to sign for them. It was a big shock. However, when he returned to Scotland to sign for Celtic at a fee of £150,000, on 6 November 1985, I was delighted. Ironically, this was four days after Aberdeen beat us 4-1 in the League at Pittodrie and Frank McDougall scored four. Mark is a good player and now a fine team-mate.

Mr Valentine cannot make any comment about the unhappiest moment of my football life because the SFA rules insist that he must stay silent. To be fair, nearly all the referees I have spoken to about this claim it is better for them to say nothing about incidents in which they have been involved.

Ah, well, I am a great believer in fair play so I asked Mark McGhee to tell his uncensored story. Here it is.

"First of all I thought Aberdeen deserved to win. In fact, I never thought at any time in the match that we would lose. However, Celtic earned our admiration for the way they fought back in the second half with ten men. It was quite something.

"We've discussed the ordering off a hundred times since I signed for Celtic. I still think I was fouled although I expected Roy to get a yellow card rather than a red one. The incident is still clear in my mind. At least, up to the point that I went down. My team-mates now think I overacted but this is not the case.

"I went past Mark Reid on the right-hand side of Hampden. Big Roy was coming towards me and I hit the ball past him. When I tried to follow, Roy caught me — I believe with his knee and shoulder. I fell and thought at first I had broken my arm. Very few could have realised the pain I was in. It remained that way until half-time when the physio attended it for most of our interval break.

"I was told later about Gordon Strachan and Doug Rougvie entering into arguments while I was on the ground but I wasn't aware of this at the time.

"Let me be honest about one point. As a professional I would do nearly anything to win a cup final but it stops short of deliberately trying to have an opponent sent off. I'm sure Roy never thought I tried to do this. When I saw that Roy was being ordered off my first reaction was that Aberdeen now had a better chance. Roy, after all, is a key player. I also felt sorry for him. Being dismissed from a cup final must be horrendous.

"That's my viewpoint but I must say there has never been any enmity about it from Roy or any other player. We talk about it regularly — mostly jokingly — and try to argue each other's case. I can remember raising the ordering off with some Celts weeks later but the chat was conducted without ill-feeling.

"I knew I was bound for Hamburg after the game and wanted to be absolutely sure that nobody could accuse me of not giving 100 per cent. That's why I was so pleased to score the winner and be awarded the 'Mr Superfit' title. The Celtic lads give me stick about this, of course.

"The winner was a volley by me at the far post but only after Dougie Bell had hit the crossbar and then Gordon Strachan flighted the ball in my direction.

"It's an odd situation. I contributed to Celtic losing the Cup, and, unwittingly, to Roy being sent off. But I am now desperate to help Celtic win everything in sight. Roy and I remain good pals. I wouldn't have expected anything else from a man of his calibre."

There my personal Hampden horror rests. My nightmare has become a historical statistic which sadly cannot be erased.

It is worth saying something here, though, about the League Cup final which took place earlier that season and which was also refereed by Mr Valentine. Agatha Christie could not have scripted more thrills or improbabilities. Celtic were very annoyed in the end. Not just because we lost 3-2 to Rangers after extra-time, but because of controversy surrounding many important events during the 120 minutes. Ally McCoist was in jubilant mood, having scored a hat-trick against Celtic in front of 66,369 people.

It was 2-2 at the end of 90 minutes. In the first period of extra-time — in 104 minutes to be precise — Mr Valentine gave a penalty against me for a tackle on McCoist a few steps inside the penalty area. McCoist took the kick and, whereas Pat Bonner had gone the wrong way for a McCoist penalty in 44 minutes, this time he lunged left and stopped the ball. But he couldn't hold it and McCoist followed up to score the winner.

We got a penalty, too, which led to the equaliser by Mark Reid a minute from half-time. The final score was a let down for us, though.

Eye on the ball, evading an outstretched boot, Roy is in full flight.

The forecasters had gone for Celtic almost to a man and we felt very confident. Tommy Burns had a particularly good game and almost succeeded in tipping the balance in our favour. However, it was not to be.

To complete our season of woe Aberdeen won the Premier League Championship. They retained it the following season and it wasn't until season 1984-85 that we recaptured the title we all covet most of all.

Chapter 6

A SOCCER LANDMARK

THE date was 18 May 1985, and the occasion the 100th Scottish Cup final. It was a time for history and Celtic realised it. It was also an appropriate 90 minutes for Davie Hay to win his first major trophy as a manager. And I was voted "Mr Superfit" after kicking off as a virtual cripple able to play only because of a pain-killing injection.

What an afternoon it was. Celtic "came back from the dead" to win 2-1 with two goals of real beauty — by Davie Provan and Frank McGarvey — which were a delight to all except Dundee United and their supporters. We had to win. Our minds were made up. But how it was to be achieved was another matter. We had been also-rans too often — three times, in fact, in the previous season.

Winning the hundredth final would be special, a landmark in football. Before we even got to Hampden, though, there was high drama behind the scenes at our favourite training place at Seamill on the Ayrshire coast, not very far from my home. I bent to pick up a cup of tea in the hotel and by some freak, injured my back. This had never happened before nor has it happened since. I could scarcely move and there was no question of me training that afternoon. It was so bad that I thought I wouldn't be able to play. What a blow that would have been, particularly to me.

The boss decided my injury had to be kept secret so the Press weren't told and I had to stay in my room. I was like a geriatric and would have been an instant give-away had they seen me.

Next morning my back had improved but not enough for me to play a few hours later. The manager was not for leaving me out, though, and I was glad of that. He decided to take me to Glasgow ahead of the team so that I could have a pain-killing injection by a specialist friend of the club. I felt my back was improving quickly but I got the injection anyway. We then drove a short distance to the MacDonald Hotel at Giffnock to await the team travelling from Seamill.

As we sat in the boss's car outside the hotel we couldn't believe our eyes. There were Jim McLean and the Dundee United players getting ready for Hampden. Unknown to us they had been staying there overnight. We had to duck down so they couldn't see us. It would have been clear to a shrewdie like Mr McLean that something must be wrong and it involved me. Thankfully, none of the United lads glimpsed me and I appeared on the pitch at Hampden as if brand new.

During the game I didn't feel a twinge and to this day I don't really know what caused the trouble. My only apprehension was when Stuart Beedie scored for United in the 54th minute. It was raining and I wondered if it was tears from above for an impending defeat for us.

That day the legions of Celtic fans were remarkable — irresistible really. Jim McLean said they were "unbelievable" and coming from a bitterly disappointed manager this was high praise. It was thoroughly deserved since they created a cauldron of noise which drove us on. But it is true to say that a club such as United, with magnificent achievements under Jim McLean, have a massive task on their hands operating against the tremendous backing given to Celtic or Rangers.

One writer described Celtic's performance that day most colourfully: "The Celts looked like death on the *Titanic* but they suddenly found the lifeboats." Our revival was inspired by a bold, a very bold, substitution by the boss. In the 74th minute he pulled off Paul McStay and replaced him with Pierce O'Leary. I was told to push forward in a final gamble to snatch the silverware from United, who were looking and playing so confidently. Tommy Burns also went off to be replaced by Brian McClair but Tommy had a hand

Roy shows his "Mr Superfit" plaque and the Scottish Cup.

injury and turned up at the after-match celebration at the Grosvenor Hotel with it in plaster.

Cheers rang out in our ears and the terracings and stands seemed to be a sea of green. How could such encouragement be resisted? The answer was, it couldn't.

Two minutes after the switch that sent me into attack, Celtic were awarded a free kick 20 yards from goal. Davie Provan and Murdo MacLeod shaped up to take it. Hamish McAlpine, in the United goal, probably thought Davie would hurdle the ball and leave it to Murdo who is well known to have a powerful shot. What Hamish didn't know was that Davie had practised this very dead-ball situation dozens of times in training during the week.

Afterwards Davie said the law of averages had been in his favour. He had missed them all in training! He certainly didn't fail with this most important shot of all. The ball zoomed over the wall and curled brilliantly under the bar only inches from Hamish's outstretched hands.

Davie could hardly believe what he had done, but no confirmation was needed by the rest of us. Referee Brian McGinlay pointed to the middle of the park. We were on level terms and there was a strong scent of victory in our nostrils. Defeat seemed — and was — out of the question. We had become a different team and the manager had to take a lot of the credit for this.

Six minutes from the end — no, I wasn't wearing a wrist watch but simply checked later! — I made a cross. It was head-high and in front of a retreating defence. Frank MGarvey launched himself instinctively at the ball and from ten yards sent it swirling into the United goal.

I've never felt so happy. With 16 minutes to go our chances didn't seem to be worth a used bus ticket. However, it's history now that we did win and in the moment of victory I think Frank was as surprised as anybody at the ease with which the ball sailed into the net. Again it wasn't far away from McAlpine's desperately grasping hands.

I'm an avid reader of the papers, listen closely to the radio and love the sports programmes on TV. I was more than happy about this Monday morning verdict: "Davie Hay's tactical switches in the second half were hugely successful when Celtic were running out of everything including hope. None was more effective than pushing forward the human dynamo Roy (The Rover) Aitken to whip Celtic home like Lester Piggott driving a reluctant winner past the post."

It was certainly a much happier aftermath for me than it had been the year before when I was sent off. However, I understood how Kevin Moran of Manchester United felt. He was sent off at Wembley in the English Cup final while we were beating Dundee United. Unlike me, though, Moran saw his mates beating Everton with a Norman Whiteside goal in extra-time.

Our victory — the club's 27th in the final — pleased me for the other reason that it gave Davie Hay confidence. Earlier he had said he might quit if he couldn't produce the success the supporters were entitled to expect. I believe he was being sincere when he said this. In the dressing-room we were happy to have adjusted his success ratio.

Davie quickly demonstrated his single-mindedness. Within a

few days Frank McGarvey was up for transfer and first moves were being made for him to join St Mirren for £80,000, exactly £180,000 less than he cost from Liverpool when he joined up at Parkhead on 11 March 1980. Frank's spell at Liverpool hadn't worked out but that was no disgrace. Liverpool frequently buy players who never make the first team as regulars. He was just one of many. However, in his five years at Parkhead he was always popular with us and the fans. He could also be depended on to get goals.

The fans were taken aback by the news that he was leaving, especially as he had just scored the winning goal in the Cup final. My view was that the time was right for him to change. Right for both him and the club. Frank was 29 and the year before he might have been transferred had the right offer been made.

I felt Frank would get new stimulus from being in fresh surroundings. Often a move can be beneficial and this is not only true of football. It happens in most other jobs. While I was sorry to see Frank going I thought at the time it was a sensible move for him and I hope he agrees with this view. Certainly, any time we've played St Mirren since Frank has been one of the players we've had to watch specially. And particularly that head of his. The one which enabled us to win the hundredth Cup final and also made a contribution to Saints fine Hampden Scottish Cup final success against Dundee United in 1986-87.

Chapter 7

FOOTBALL CAME SECOND

TROUBLE at Old Firm cup finals has too often overshadowed the football. This is something players regret even more than the decent fans who have always been very much in the majority. I believe the game should not be influenced by outside matters such as bigotry which can be the basis for hatred.

Mounted police, one a woman, became front-page news after the final on 11 May 1980. Celts won the Cup for a record 26th time in our 41st final, with a goal by George McCluskey. But for the next week all I read about was the trouble which flared at the end of extra-time. The violence as fighting fans of both teams swarmed on to Hampden was described as the worst for 70 years. The mounties drew their long batons as they were brought on as a last resort to put an end to the trouble. In the dressing-room we were blissfully unaware of what was going on. We were busily drinking the bubbly.

The final tally of arrests was 160, with a further 50 held for incidents outside the ground. I quote this to remind us all how much better the behaviour of fans has been since the introduction of the Criminal Justice (Scotland) Bill which has had an important effect on crowd reaction. Pleas by Celtic and Rangers in the clubs' newspapers have also helped. The *Celtic View* has implored fans consistently to watch it and I feel the message has been driven home.

Although nothing is ever certain in the area of crowd behaviour I think the marked improvement will be maintained.

Kenny Dalglish said at the time of our final: "The game was good and exciting and deserves to be remembered as such. I was saddened, though, by the actions of fans. This final merited something better than the unruly actions resulting in terrible scenes at the end." This was an opinion with which I agreed completely.

Celtic went into the game severely handicapped because Roddie MacDonald and Tom McAdam, our two out and out centre-halves, were suspended. Billy McNeill decided that Mike Conroy would be centre-half with me alongside. It took our supporters by surprise but Mike finished as the game's outstanding performer.

Celtic were given very little chance. Rangers had acknowledged strength in the air provided by players like Derek Johnstone and Colin Jackson who moved forward in support when free kicks were being taken. Mike was given the job of marking Johnstone. The experts seemed to think there would be only one winner and he was in a blue shirt — *they* thought! In fact, I don't think Big Derek got one ball in the air, so well did Mike play in his unaccustomed role. He deserved to be the man of the match.

Another guy who played well was our goalie Peter Latchford. He was told he would have to come out to help us because it was true we didn't have enough height at the back.

It was a good final. A lot of end-to-end play made it thrilling for the customers although the 90 minutes was goalless. And so to extra-time. We had just moved into the second stage of that when the ball broke to Danny McGrain. He smacked it towards the goal. Peter McCloy took a couple of steps towards his right-hand post. George McCluskey stuck out a foot and sent the ball careering into the net. Peter went one way and the ball the other.

The last kick of the game was a ball floated into our box. Latchford came above us all, caught it and as he did so the final whistle went. Peter's right arm was up in the air in a victory salute while he had the ball tucked under the other one. I'll never forget the look of pleasure on his face as he waved to the fans.

We were the underdogs. It's the way I prefer it because, in a sense, the pressure is off a wee bit. The crowd expect so much from the favourites and being "written down" is a spur to the players' pride. It really gets us going.

Jim Baxter was aggrieved at Rangers performance as the

favourites. He called them a "scandal" and said they hadn't competed. Pat Crerand, on the other hand, was happy with Celtic and, incidentally, thought yours truly had played well with Mike Conroy. The teams that day were— *Celtic:* Latchford, Sneddon, Aitken, Conroy, McGrain, Provan, MacLeod, Burns, Doyle, McCluskey, McGarvey. Lennox used as sub. *Rangers:* McCloy, Stevens, Jackson, Forsyth, Dawson, Jardine, Russell, Smith, Cooper, Johnstone, MacDonald. McLean and Miller subs.

Completing my Scottish Cup final treble — although actually it was the first — was our 1-0 victory on 7 May 1977. We had already won the League with a victory at Easter Road, where Joe Craig was our scorer. It was my first season as a full-timer and I was still only 18, but I was being paid £60 a week plus bonuses. It was good money and I knew it. More important, though, was the experience that I, as an up-and-coming lad, was gaining from company which included Kenny Dalglish, Danny McGrain, Pat Stanton and Johannes Edvaldsson.

Jock Stein had taken us to the Marine Hotel in Troon for a few days' preparation before the match and our victory was really a triumph for Stein's tactics. The marking was exceptionally tight and creative men like Dalglish and Tommy McLean were contained. Edvaldsson frustrated Derek Johnstone completely every time the ball came near them in the air. Roddie MacDonald also finished up the best player on the park.

We won through a controversial penalty scored by Andy Lynch in the 20th minute. The penalty incident could be traced right back to Stewart Kennedy injuring himself by hitting a post while stopping a Lynch header. The 'keeper needed treatment and the sponge had hardly been put away when Alfie Conn took a corner on the left. Up went Big Roddie to meet the cross with his head. It spun to Edvaldsson who immediately hit it towards goal. Kennedy stopped it a yard from the goal, with Sandy Jardine and Johnstone covering on the line behind him. The ball came back off the big Icelander and Bob Valentine, the referee, said Johnstone used a hand and not his knee to stop it crossing the line.

Penalty! There was consternation all around. Kenny Dalglish was supposed to take the penalties but just didn't feel good about taking this one. Andy Lynch volunteered to take the kick and he had blasted it past Kennedy with his left foot before anybody could argue. "Shuggy" claims to this day that "DJ" caught the ball with his hand

but Rangers to a man said it was his knee. Television pictures were inconclusive and only fuelled arguments. As Jock Stein once said about watching TV replays with a partisan eye: "You see what you want to see." I suspect this was the case with supporters of both Celtic and Rangers. None, as is well known, are more partisan. So far as we were concerned there was no doubt. Johnstone was guilty of handling and Lynch was our hero with his first penalty goal for Celtic. The teams were — *Celtic*: Latchford, McGrain, Stanton, MacDonald, Edvaldsson, Lynch, Conn, Dalglish, Aitken, Craig, Wilson. *Rangers:* Kennedy, Jardine, Forsyth, Jackson, Greig, Hamilton, Watson, MacDonald, McLean, Parlane, Johnstone. Robertson used as sub.

Chapter 8

GAME THAT HAD EVERYTHING

I'VE played in 47 Old Firm games — won 21 and lost 11 — up until the end of season 1986/87 but far and away the most exciting was on 21 May 1979. That was the day we beat Rangers 4-2 at Parkhead and it was a game which had everything. A crowd of 52,000 probably haven't had such football excitement since.

Let me remind you of the scene. In February of that season it had looked as though we were way out of the title race. I have to admit that at that stage we looked like also-rans. The forecasting pundits were certainly going "gaga" about Rangers' chances. A lot of our matches had been postponed because of bad weather which further complicated the position and catching up became a worry.

However, in spite of the problems, Celtic had done remarkably well. So much so that going into this, our last fixture of the season, we were three points ahead of Rangers who still had to play Partick Thistle and Hibs. A victory meant we would be champions. We had done our sums about the effect of a draw and realised without too much adding and subtracting that this wouldn't be good enough, as Rangers had a better goal difference. The ground was mobbed and it seemed to us there were more of our supporters, judging from the sea of green and white. It turned out to be a game which vindicated Scottish football and Old Firm meetings. It must rank as one of the most dramatically exciting ever played in Britain. If Terry Butcher, Chris Woods and Graham Roberts had been around at the time they would not have been expressing pleasant surprise at the quality of the game in Scotland. They would have known! The teams are worth recalling — *Celtic*: Latchford, McGrain, Lynch, Aitken, McAdam, Edvaldsson, Provan, Conroy, McCluskey, MacLeod, Doyle. *Rangers:* McCloy, Jardine, Dawson, Johnstone, Jackson, MacDonald, McLean, Russell, Parlane, Smith, Cooper.

Billy McNeill was in search of his first league title as Parkhead manager but when Alex MacDonald — the same skilful guy who's now manager of Hearts — scored for Rangers in nine minutes he must have wondered what was happening. It was an uphill fight but I have never been in a team which showed such outright commitment. The same could be said about Rangers. They have never played better in any of the matches I've been involved in with them. This gives you an idea of why it was such a smashing contest.

Luck seemed to be against us. Very much so. At half-time, 1-0 down, it looked as though our whole season was to end in a shambles. However, nobody said or thought this among the players and when we went out again it was clear that our fans realised the importance of giving us their backing. There was a constant buzz of noise from our area of the stand and terracings. Before half-time Johnny Doyle was sent off. I didn't see the incident which took place near the players' entrance at Parkhead. A linesman thought Johnny had kicked MacDonald as he lay on the ground. Doyle's explanation later was that he thought MacDonald was overacting and he made a gesture to back up his plea for him to get on his feet. Eddie Pringle, from Edinburgh, now retired from refereeing, went to his linesman, heard his version and a hushed crowd then saw us being reduced to ten men as Johnny was sent off.

We were trying anxiously to get ourselves together after Doyle's expulsion and determination paid off more quickly than we expected or even dared to hope. I equalised and if it wasn't the best goal I've ever scored it was certainly the best and most timely contribution I've been able to make to any game. The ball cannoned from somebody's foot — I've never found out who the anonymous player was — and when it broke to my left I turned it in past Peter McCloy. It was 1-1 and we were back in the game.

George McCluskey volleyed a second goal for us in 74 minutes. By this time our fans were going bananas and we were doing our best on

A goal against Rangers and Roy leaps to celebrate with Peter McCloy on his knees.

the pitch not to do the same. The game swung our way astonishingly. Even Rangers seemed to forget we had only ten men. It was more like 12, the amount of running each player — particularly Davie Provan — did.

Eight minutes to go and Rangers forced a corner. The ball was floated wide but in line with the back post. It beat everybody. Standing at the corner of the box was Bobby Russell and you can imagine what happened next. There must have been 18 players crowded in the box but Russell's volley passed every one of us and tucked itself into the far corner. So that was 2-2 with under ten minutes to go.

Our position was desperate but back we went at the Rangers defence once again. George McCluskey, almost miraculously, set up a goal although technically the credit went to Colin Jackson who would much rather not have had the dubious honour. George smacked the ball across the goal with his right foot and it bounced obligingly off Jackson's back. McCloy had moved off his line and I was in front of him by this time. The ball bounced and bounced again and rolled awkwardly over the line. McCloy tried to get back to stop it but I had the satisfaction of knowing he had to get past me first.

I certainly had the best view possible of the goal but, if anything, the fourth was even more memorable. It was scored by Murdo MacLeod in the last few seconds. He got the ball 35 yards out and hit it beautifully into the "postage-stamp corner" of McCloy's goal with his powerful right foot. I don't think I've ever seen anybody looking so pleased about anything. Murdo went down on his knees in front of the stand. My dad and my wife were sitting in the stand and told me later that they had never seen joy like it. The fans stood up on the seats and then began jumping up and down with delight.

It was far and away the best game I've played in, better even than beating Dundee United in the Cup or winning the League on the last day of season 1985-86. We felt drained at the end of the match but if ever 90 minutes of super effort was worth it this was it.

I looked at the faces of some of our supporters on the way to the dressing-room. Their smiles and laughing eyes were the ultimate in happiness. It was the highlight of my career. A game I'll never forget any more, I suppose, than those thousands of fans who watched such a Titanic struggle.

Chapter 9

THE INFLUENCE OF 'FERGIE'

I OWE a debt of gratitude to Alex Ferguson as he played a considerable part in my international revival along with Jock Stein. In fact, I played more international matches in a year under them than I did in the first five years of my international career. I always felt that Fergie influenced big Jock in my comeback.

Anyway, after playing in the first of the Rous Cup games against England I was in every match before Mexico and during it, with the exception of a friendly in Holland, when I was needed by Celtic and Scotland excused me since the game was not an important international.

So I always think affectionately of Fergie. He had a reputation as a club manager for being ruthless but at international level and especially during the World Cup games we never saw any evidence of this. He treated us well. There was never any bother. Everything was straighforward to him. His team talks were very much to the point and no player could say after a game they weren't warned about any important aspect of the opposing team's play.

Perhaps his matey approach to the World Cup job was because he knew, and always said, that he would go back to Aberdeen after Mexico and quit the international scene. Well, we all know he eventually joined Manchester United where I think he will bring

The Tony McGuinness Cup which Celtic won and Roy shakes with Alex Ferguson, Arthur Albiston and Gordon Strachan look on.

success back to Old Trafford and increase his already considerable stature. He also did me the honour of taking United north to play in my testimonial match. When he was asked to provide the opposition Fergie didn't hesitate, which was flattering to me. However, I would not rule him out of going back to the Scotland job in the years ahead. The bigger the platform the better for him.

In a sense Fergie was like a team-mate. The only time I felt he was under pressure was when he was picking teams. He found it difficult to leave players out and he talked to the Press about "the hardest decision of my life . . . I hated it". All the same, Fergie had a good way of handling disappointments for players.

He has a nervous cough which becomes more obvious at tricky moments. Sometimes we would hear the cough before we saw the manager and we'd go into hiding. We knew that if he wanted to speak to a player, especially before any of the three World Cup ties against Denmark, West Germany and Uruguay, it was to explain

Training with Scotland . . . Pat Nevin, Gordon Strachan, Roy, Murdo MacLeod and Raymond Stewart.

why he wasn't playing. The individual was always the first to know — and why. It was a good system and I was fortunate, very much so, never to have had one of these pre-game explanations because I was in all three ties. However, it is better to know in advance if you are dropped. It could be embarrassing to find out in the middle of a team talk with 20 or so players in the room.

Jock Stein wouldn't do this. He announced a side and then left the choice of five subs until just before the games. In the dressing-room he would read out five names and the ones left out just had to sneak out of the place. There was never any explanation, at least not to me.

It is simply a matter of style and in this particular aspect I feel Alex Ferguson had it right.

I remember particularly the night before our game with the infamous Uruguay. The cough was worse than I had heard it. Fergie knew, for instance, he had to tell Alex McLeish he wasn't playing. Big Alex was ill before the West German match and the manager decided he wasn't ready for the Uruguayans. It must have been very hard for him to say this to one of his best Aberdeen club men. Alex was down in the mouth but accepted that David Narey and Willie Miller should keep their places.

The big decision, however, was the omission of Graeme Souness. He had spoken with Fergie after the West Germany game. I think he felt the pace a bit in the rarefied air. Graeme was told the night before he wouldn't be playing in our third match. It was another of these decisions which Fergie disliked but had to make. That's what managers are for.

Although Graeme had talked with the manager he was upset when told he was out. After all, he was the team captain. There was no argument. Nothing like that at all. I felt that Graeme and Fergie had too much respect for each other to row about it. My view was that Graeme accepted the fact that he was dropped like any other professional. He was dejected.

By the way, I think it's worth saying as a Celtic man that I've always been friendly with Graeme on Scotland trips. In fact, I shared a room with him for a week. He goes out of his way to speak to other players. I also envied his stylish cases with his clothes beautifully packed. Graeme always had the very best gear. I found him to be a perfect gentleman and have a lot of time for him despite the fact that in Old Firm games we are on opposite sides.

Graeme is sometimes accused of being aloof. I have never found him to be this way. When I first met him he played for Liverpool and then Sampdoria in Italy. He is very cosmopolitan and after his move to Rangers I noticed no difference in his attitude to the other players, although he had become a manager.

This brings me on to another point of fascination for the fans. There is a mistaken idea among the supporters that off the pitch Celtic and Rangers players don't get along. It's nonsense, even though Graeme and I would expect each other to be 100 per cent in opposition when our clubs meet and I certainly wouldn't regard him as the perfect gentleman on the pitch! As captain of Celtic I've met my Rangers opposite number Terry Butcher several times for photo sessions or at functions involving both clubs. Terry couldn't have been more pleasant, although like myself he doesn't like losing games.

To get back to the subject of the 1986 World Cup, another player who was especially disappointed not to kick off in the last match in Mexico was Frank McAvennie. He had been playing so well for West Ham and Scotland that he was rated a certainty for more than one of our games, particularly as the front positions had proved to be problematic because the lads weren't getting goals. So Frank

Miss World 1986 matches the smiles of Roy and Terry Butcher at a charity function.

obviously had high hopes of kicking off against Uruguay. Instead that honour went to Graeme Sharp and Paul Sturrock, with Charlie Nicholas appearing in the last 20 minutes. Like the others not playing, it wasn't hard to see Frank was unhappy but he too realised that the manager had a difficult choice to make.

Our World Cup adventure began on the Santa Fe trail. We lived in the town where Billy the Kid and Jesse James once rested up after roaming the prairies of what is now New Mexico. The purpose of our 14-day stay was to prepare for the high altitude of Mexico itself. It was a worthwhile exercise. Facilities at the Sheraton Hotel were excellent and the atmosphere was nicely relaxed. In the past Scots teams haven't reacted too well to being away from home for long periods, but this was like a working holiday.

It was unfortunate that when we arrived some TV reports emphasised this more than we would have liked. Northern Ireland were filmed running up hills about 50 miles away from us at Albuquerque and England sweated in a training game. When the cameras panned to the Scots we were lazing by the luxurious hotel swimming pool and were presented like rich holidaymakers. I phoned home for the first time to be told this by my wife who thought it was a great joke. In fact the truth behind the television pictures was that when the cameramen arrived we were not long ahead of them after a long flight from London. The manager had given us a day's complete rest and it was during this period that we were filmed.

It looked particularly bad as Billy Bingham was really working Northern Ireland very hard and there was even controversy at home in Belfast about whether or not they were doing too much. An image of lazing tourists was the last one we wanted to establish, having won back credibility in Spain four years before, after the shambles of Argentina when highly coloured tales were sent home.

Matters were made worse when we were asked to attend a reception thrown by, of all things, local American clansmen, some of whom had never even seen Scotland. A photographer appeared and pictured Paul Sturrock with a glass in hand. The fact that it contained lemonade was irrelevant. The caption said, "Elbow-bending exercise for the Scots!" A picture agency got hold of it and Paul's photo was sent around the world, hinting that this was the Scots on the rampage again.

Alex Ferguson was furious. The photographer appeared innocently at our training next morning to be told off sharply by the manager. The American genuinely hadn't realised the interpretation which could be put on the picture. He apologised.

I can say that we worked very hard in Santa Fe. It was a quiet place, exactly what we wanted. We were very far from being tourists. Fergie even persuaded a reluctant Billy Bingham to bring his Northern Ireland team out of the posh Hilton Hotel at Albuquerque to play us in an 80-minute bounce match. The Irish team included John McClelland, the ex-Ranger, so I think it made him feel good to hear Scots voices again. It was an enjoyable no-tackling affair which ended 6-6. But Richard Gough unhappily got a bang on the face in a collision with Leicester City's John O'Neill. Fortunately Richard recovered quickly and it didn't affect his play in the World Cup.

The Wild West of Canada during a Scotland trip and guess who these hombres are . . . Roy and Mark McGhee have the cards and Gordon Strachan and Tommy Burns look on.

Dr Stewart Hillis was constantly making medical checks on each player before and after training. Each session on the training pitch had a purpose. The local people put up a huge banner saying "Welcome, Scotland" and they also came in their hundreds to watch us in preparation. Even superstar Robert Redford, who has a home in Santa Fe, popped into the hotel briefly, though I didn't see him.

Fergie set the right tone. There wasn't a "them" and "us" attitude between players, staff and officials. The manager himself was very much one of the boys although we were always aware that in the last analysis he was the gaffer. Walter Smith, Archie Knox, Craig Brown and Andy Roxburgh mixed in with the lads. Charlie Nicholas, as usual, was the joker of our pack. To ensure that there were no cliques, which can be a bad thing in a travelling party, players were allocated different seats for each meal so that we were always sitting next to another team-mate. Everybody got along fine. There was no hassle. Nor should there have been as we had everything a team could have wanted.

The SFA Secretary, Ernie Walker, had gone out a couple of times before the World Cup finals to pick the hotels and he certainly made a good job of it. In the evenings we dined on a verandah overlooking the Santa Fe valley. We couldn't actually see it, of course, but the Grand Canyon was only about 20 miles away. There was an Indian Reservation, too, but really not a lot to see there. Mostly they wanted to sell Indian crafts. However, I was amused to be told that one young Indian boy was called Scot MacDonald, but his Mum, sensing disappointment, pointed out that he was the son of Chief Running Water.

Before we finally went to Mexico — we were the last of 24 countries to arrive and were criticised in some quarters for it — we played matches against Los Angeles Heat and Los Angeles Kickers. The purpose was really medical. Dr Hillis said that after training at altitude players lost a bit of their fitness so we had a really hard session that day before we met Heat. LA is, of course, at sea level.

We felt really tired in the capital city of soap opera, where "JR" and Joan Collins make *Dallas* and *Dynasty*. Rod Stewart wanted to throw a party for the team there, but the manager wouldn't hear of it. I went shopping among the millionaires of Beverly Hills just to say I had been there. In the end, though, it was a relief to get to Mexico. The action, the real Mackay, was about to begin.

We stayed in a beautiful setting about 40 miles out of Mexico City in a 40-room hotel at the foot of the Mexican Pyramids where the brochures said, "Men become gods". The staff all turned out, playing Mexican music, when we drove up, heavily escorted in an air-conditioned luxury coach with tinted windows. There was always a fleet of police cars in front and behind the bus with an ambulance and team of medicos. It was very impressive. I'd never seen anything like it.

The hotel had only one telephone, so it was difficult even to make calls home which the SFA allowed us. Above all we had privacy. Nobody could get near us without permission. There were police guards everywhere. Friendly Mexican cops, but I wouldn't like to have got on the wrong side of them.

Mexico is a strange mixture of the very poor and the very well-off. Apart from evidence of the earthquake which had hit the stricken country a year before, there was a vast shanty town around Neza where we had to play two of our games. I have never seen such poverty. Families lived in what was really only four sheets of corrugated iron stuck together. The Mexican people, despite this, gave us a splendid reception. But we had the feeling that the poor people never saw matches, even on TV, and wanted no part of what must have seemed super-extravagance from their grubby, tattered existence. However, I believe the World Cup in Mexico can be judged successful because people around the world enjoyed the games.

Our misfortune was to be in the "Group of Death" and Scotland's passing from the tournament was to be extremely painful. The truth is if we had played half as well as we did in the first two games against better opposition we would have beaten Uruguay for sure.

I considered Jim Leighton to be Scotland's outstanding player in the three matches. Willie Miller was also superb and so was Gordon Strachan, our only scorer despite what I may think about my "goal". Everything about Leighton was *par excellence*. He exuded confidence, Miller was simply "Mr Consistent" and Strachan was a Scottish terrier with style and skill. All the lads, of course, gave their lot but these three were tops.

Argentina were the best team in the competition and Diego Maradona was the No. 1 player. I'm not surprised he earns £10,000 per week with Naples. Significantly Argentina were also top scorers with 14 goals, two more than France and Russia. When it really came to the crunch Maradona, who got five goals, put the ball in the back of the net when it counted most.

In the final with West Germany, Maradona was naturally built up as the star, the man to cause all the problems. Because of this he took the pressure off his team-mates. Maradona dragged defenders every way and the man who profited most was Jorge Burruchaga. He finally ran through the West German defence and guided his shot into the back of the net to give Argentina a second World Cup triumph in eight years with a 3-2 victory.

My admiration for Maradona is unstinted. Even when he punched in the first of two goals against England in a 2-1 defeat for Bobby Robson's side at the fabulous Aztec Stadium in front of 114,580. That first one was a cheat but the second goal was sheer magic. One balanced the other. It would have been unrealistic to expect Maradona or any other player, taking unfair advantage in a split-second, to go to the referee afterwards and ask for the goal to be disallowed. The Tunisian official, Ben Nasser, would probably have collapsed instead of merely having to look at TV replays later and wonder how he managed to miss the scoring punch.

Maradona said later that the controversial goal was "a little bit of the hand of God and the head of Diego". Only he could get away with such a claim. Anyway, I don't think we will ever see total honesty in these situations. With so much at stake it is naïve to expect it. Corinthian attitudes have long since departed from the sporting scene, and especially in the World Cup.

Chapter 10

THE INSIDE ON MEXICO

OUR first real sight of the World Cup was England losing 1-0 to a Carlos Manuel goal for Portugal in Monterrey. The Scots party were watching in the TV room of the Arquelogicas Hotel which was our HQ in Mexico. I must confess there was a lot of cheering from us, and particularly by the lads who play in England. Good natured stuff, of course!

Next day it was our turn to meet Denmark, who were playing in their first World Cup finals while Scotland were there for the fourth time in a row. And no doubt Bryan Robson and company were giving *us* raspberries.

We were at the ground, heavily escorted, two hours from the kick-off. We knew the Danes were probably the most cavalier country since the spectacular Holland team of the seventies. Denmark, we found out right away, were leaving out Jan Molby because he had said he didn't feel fully fit and recalling Jesper Olsen. But in Preben Elkjaer and Michael Laudrup they had what was widely recognised as the best striking partnership in Europe at that time.

For our part the absence of Kenny Dalglish, who called off with injury just before our party departed from Scotland, left Alex Ferguson with no recognised striking partnership and certainly no marksmen who had been getting goals at international level. Before we left home it was believed Frank McAvennie was certain to play, but Fergie now decided to field Charlie Nicholas along with Paul Sturrock because of their training performances.

The first thing which struck me was the atmosphere. There was a posse of Scots, maybe about 2,000, but in total the crowd was only 18,000. In a World Cup tie we had expected the ground to be packed.

We played a 4-4-2 system with Steve Nicol and Eamonn Bannon wide in the middle. We were aware that the Danes like man for man marking, with three defenders in the middle controlled by the veteran Morten Olsen as spare man. Scotland's idea was that Paul Sturrock could revel in spaces created behind the defenders. He's great at running off the ball and, of course, with Charlie Nicholas's control so good the situation seemed tailor-made for them.

It was a very even first half and could have gone either way. Both teams concentrated on sussing each other out. I recall in the second half Willie Miller had a couple of great tackles on Frank Arnesen and Preben Elkjaer.

We decided to push forward which may have been a mistake. After the two Miller tackles we should have "sat in" for ten or 15 minutes and then taken stock. Instead, in moving up we created a gap between the back four and the midfield. Arnesen got a lot of room because of this. It was Arnesen who ran down our right flank and made the pass to Ellijaer. Miller never actually got a tackle on him. Instead the ball cannoned off Willie's legs to the Dane. Elkjaer's scoring shot went in off the bottom of the far post.

It's not a pleasant feeling to see the ball going into your goal — in any game, that is, but much worse in the World Cup.

The manager brought on Eamonn Bannon for Gordon Strachan in 74 minutes but before this Charlie Nicholas was badly fouled and had to be replaced by Frank McAvennie. Klaus Bergeren was booked by the Hungarian referee, Lajos Nemeth, for that foul and Charlie had to miss our next game and in fact played only the last 20 minutes of the final match. Fergie's strategy was considerably upset as he felt Charlie was just running into scoring form.

I thought I had scored midway through the second half and I still do for that matter. It seems television back home appeared to prove there was nothing wrong with my "goal". The ball broke to Miller at the corner of the 18-yard line. He flighted it in perfectly and I remember Richard Gough and I both going for it. I chested it down and hit it first time. Just as I whacked the ball, I heard the whistle and the linesman's flag was up.

Jesper Olsen who played so well for Denmark in the Mexico World Cup.

The only explanation I could get afterwards was that Charlie, just before he had to go off, was late coming out after an attack and was stranded offside as I made my shot. However, many people made the point that Charlie couldn't have been interfering with play. It is a very difficult decision for a referee. At the time I didn't argue. The first thing to do in a match of this importance is get back into position. Arguing with the referee is pointless. However, I've watched the move again on TV and can see nothing wrong. Roy Aitken should have appeared on the score-sheet and, as the section worked out, this would have put us into the next phase for the first time in history.

We were against top opposition in Denmark. But our back four of Gough, McLeish, Miller and Malpas were very solid. I really did think — and not because I "scored" — that we deserved to get a draw with Denmark. As I swopped jerseys with Arnesen at the end of the game I was not to know that the result of that first World Cup tie would be the unluckiest of the three. Just for the record the teams were — *Scotland:* Leighton, Gough, Malpas, Souness, McLeish, Miller, Strachan (Bannon 74), Aitken, Nicol, Nicholas (McAvennie 61), Sturrock. *Denmark:* Rasmussen, Busk, M. Olsen, Nielsen, Lerby, J. Olsen, Bergeren, Elkjaer, Laudrup, Bertelsen, Arnesen.

We played our second game against West Germany at Queretaro and the heat was a burning 80 degrees. Although we were seeing blue skies for the first time it was really sweltering. Queretaro is a splendid old Spanish colonial town and 25,000 at Corregidora stadium certainly gave the place a bit of atmosphere.

There had been a lot of stories about the West German Press going to town on Franz Beckenbauer's team after their drawing 1-1 with Uruguay. Manager Ferguson was given a first-hand report of this match and had been told that, apart from man-marking, Peter Briegel on one side and Thomas Berthold on the other were great on the overlaps. The system was really much the same as the Danes played except that the West Germans were much more experienced at this level. And they had the fox himself, Beckenbauer, doing the planning. He made one change, bringing in Pierre Littbarski in place of Andreas Brehme.

Scotland were forced to call on Dave Narey because Alex McLeish was down with a bad flu. He was the only one among the Scots players to be affected in any way during our jaunt to America and Mexico, which speaks highly of the way we were looked after. Fergie

Determination from Roy in a Scotland jersey but Glen Hoddle shields the ball cleverly.

also had to change the strikers. He elected to have only one man up front, Steve Archibald, and put Eamonn Bannon into the midfield. It was also decided that Gordon Strachan would play in front of the midfield and behind Archibald.

The idea worked well, particularly in the early stages of an exciting match. Gordon was outstanding but I feel Archibald got little praise for the work he did. He didn't get a lot of touches of the ball but still worked tremendously hard pulling defenders with him. He had been used to this kind of slog playing with Barcelona in Spain. Steve hasn't been too popular with Scots fans but on this blistering afternoon I made him one of our best. It was a rotten and unpopular job and especially against opposition of this class. Steve did it well.

When wee Gordon eventually scored a goal against the West Germans — our only one in three games — I'm happy to say I put the ball through to him. Having gone ahead against a team of West Germany's calibre — they did after all get to the final — I now thought to myself we had a chance and a very real one. We hadn't forgotten that the Germans were strong and disciplined. But, sad to say, they didn't give us time to consolidate after getting in front.

Five minutes later Littbarski threaded a pass down the left to Klaus Allofs. He battered the ball across the goal from the by-line to beat Leighton, a rare happening in the World Cup games, and Rudi Voller knocked it into an empty goal. Although Strachan continued to make German hearts flutter we had our work cut out with the runs of Briegel. We had expected them but this didn't help very much when he came at us. Then Leighton had a very fine save just before half-time. Voller ran through with only big Jim to beat but the Dons' goalkeeper cut the angle sharply enough to make a super save.

Immediately after half-time is always a dangerous period and it certainly was for us on this occasion. In fact we saw all our hopes crumbling as we sweated in front of a boisterous crowd. Dave Narey tackled Voller inside the area. As the German tumbled the ball bounced off Dave's foot into the path of Allofs. He was perfectly positioned close to the penalty spot and Leighton had no chance.

The goal was a bad blow for us. Ten minutes later McAvennie came on in place of Steve Nicol but the Germans countered this by replacing the attack-minded Briegel with Ditmar Jacobs. Later still Davie Cooper came on in place of Bannon and the Germans replaced Littbarski with Karl-Heinz Rummenigge.

I think a few of us felt the pace of the match but of the three games this was the best atmosphere. The stadium was like a Roman Coliseum but the Scottish Lion didn't roar long enough. Graeme Souness was one of the players who felt it in the heat and altitude. Even so, I reckon Graeme is still among the best midfielders in the world. He has proved himself with Liverpool, in Italy with Sampdoria, in the Scotland side and now with Rangers. He can handle the different types of play no bother. England and, indeed, the Premier League, are hell for leather, but he copes with it. To remind you, the teams were — *Scotland:* Leighton, Gough, Malpas, Souness, Miller, Strachan, Aitken, Bannon, Nicol, Narey, Archibald. *West Germany:* Schumacher, Briegel, Foerster, Eder, Littbarski, Mattheus, Voller, Magath, Berthold, Augenthaler, Allofs.

A clearance the Aitken way.

While we were failing in Queretaro, Elkjaer was grabbing a hat-trick for Denmark in a staggering 6-1 victory over Uruguay. There was an ominous warning for Scotland there because Miguel Rossio was ordered off early in the game. However, even with 11 men it's doubtful if Uruguay would have done much better against a Danish side with so much power and flair.

Five days later Scotland were back in Neza for the final game. And the remarkable thing was the Scots all knew that a win would put us through as a third-placed country. So the first two games literally didn't mean anything. It was down to us against a Uruguayan side whom everyone thought were cynical soccer hooligans.

It is history that it was a useless goalless draw and Scotland were on the way home next day, bitterly reflecting on how near and yet how far we had been. Omar Borras, the Uruguayan coach, was the man who called Group E "the Group of Death" and it seemed he had some advance knowledge. The Uruguayans shamed themselves and the competition. FIFA fined and warned them that they could be thrown out it they didn't behave.

Jose Batista was sent off in 40 seconds, the fastest ever red-carding in the World Cup. His tackle on Gordon Strachan was a deliberate attempt to maim. I do not think he had any intention of going for the ball. Referee Quiniou, of France, plucked out his red card and sent the Uruguayan off. Some supporters thought he had made a mistake and pulled out the wrong card. But there was malice in the tackle. Had it been made in a Glasgow street Batista would have landed in jail. From where I was the referee did exactly the right thing. In fact, I thought he had no option.

Instead of helping us, playing against ten men was a handicap. Uruguay simply played 4-4-1 and the front man, Francescoli, did a remarkable amount of work. I admired him, although the style of play of Uruguay was terrible. They had a lot of skill and did not need to approach the game as they did.

It is true to say Scotland will never have a better chance of going on to the next phase. With McLeish and Souness out Fergie included Paul McStay and Graeme Sharp. The moment I most remember in the game, apart from the sending off, was a chance which fell to Steve Nicol. Strachan sent me away on the right and my cross found Nicol on the six-yard line. It looked an easy one — they always do! — but Steve tried to side-foot the ball and played it into the hands of goalie Fernando Alvez. It is also true to say Leighton made one of the best saves of his life. Wilmar Cabrera's header off a free kick looked a certain goal. But big Jim made an outstanding save — his best in Mexico. My room-mate Paul McStay did rather well too. It was a hard game to come into but he performed well in the role allocated to Souness.

Having disposed of the ordering off and one terrible challenge on Paul Sturrock which he rode, I don't think Uruguay were as bad as some said. They were being judged on their reputation, coupled with the fact that they knocked us out of the World Cup. The combination had a lethal effect on our opinions.

One of the terrible statistics was that there were only around 30 minutes of actual play because of the stoppages. The referee decided he had done his job with the sending off.

My team-mates will not thank me for the reminder but here were the teams — *Scotland:* Leighton, Gough, Miller, Narey, Albiston, Aitken, Strachan, McStay, Nicol (Cooper 70), Sharp, Sturrock (Nicholoas 70). *Uruguay:* Alves, Gutierrez, Acevedo, Diego, Pereira, Batista, Ramos, Barrios, Cabrera, Francescoli, Santin.

I believe now that if we had to play the same three countries over again Scotland — and not Uruguay — would have gone into the second round.

Uruguay went through to meet Argentina and the last time the two traditional River Plate rivals had met was in the inaugural World Cup final in 1930. The Argies lost that one 4-2 but, with Maradona in great form, there was never much chance of Uruguay repeating their victory. Pedro Pasculli scored before half-time but the game finished in an electrical storm which blotted out nearby hills and ripped through the stadium. Uruguay "won" 4-3 in bookings by the splendid Italian referee — imagine me saying such a thing about a ref! — Agnolin. Next morning Uruguay were on their way home, having lost 1-0.

Chapter 11

HOW TV IMPROVED

ONE good thing about Terry Butcher, Graham Roberts and Chris Woods playing at Ibrox is that Scottish football gets a better deal from national television. Bob Wilson's *Football Focus* on BBC and ITV's *Saint and Greavsie* show dismissed the game in Scotland in a few seconds — unless Jimmy Greaves or Bob Wilson were slating Alan Rough, Billy Thomson or one of our other goalies. Television from London treated Scottish football and those involved in it as second-class citizens. However, interest has heightened with such well-known English stars in Rangers jerseys and Scotland is getting much more air time. This can only be a good thing. TV is an important part of our lives and getting major projection across the country is vital.

It is a left-handed way to achieve it, mind you. Scots teams have held up well against clubs from England, both in European and friendly games, so there was no need for the TV moguls to be so snooty. I am not blaming Bob Wilson, Ian St John or Jimmy Greaves for the scant coverage. However, the producers responsible had clearly never heard of Hampden, far less Parkhead, Ibrox, Pittodrie, Tannadice or Tynecastle. Messrs Butcher, Roberts and Woods have done some public relations missionary work as well as performing well for Rangers. I hope in future years to see even more coverage

Steve Davis watch out . . . Roy and Terry Butcher at the snooker table.

from Scotland on national TV and I don't just mean for Celtic and Rangers.

Why did Graeme Souness have to spend £2½ million to get his dream team going in the Premier League? My view is that they had fallen so far behind in face of increased competition from Aberdeen, Dundee United and Hearts — apart at all from Celtic — that they really had to spend massively. Rangers decided they needed instant action. And the Ibrox fans agree it was the right thing to do judged on the numbers flocking back to see them. It is astonishing, and heartening, that quite often games at Parkhead and Ibrox are seen by the biggest crowds in Britain.

Celtic will always compete on the transfer market but at reasonable prices. The facelift necessary at Ibrox was needed because of consistency at Parkhead over the last 20 years. However, Celtic cannot, and will not, be complacent as has been proved by the return of Billy McNeill. There have been calls for major changes in the Celtic shareholding but the club will move carefully and wisely going into the centenary year in 1988.

The Premier League has been good for Scottish clubs, including Celtic. It has also seen a very much more intensive challenge from Aberdeen and Dundee United. Players from these clubs have proved the most difficult opponents for me over the years — in particular Paul Sturrock and Mark McGhee, although he is now a team-mate with Celtic. Both work extremely hard and move about the pitch a great deal. A forward playing in front of you is obviously easier to mark. Sturrock plays off a defender and McGhee is good at making runs away from you. They are difficult to pick up. The big, orthodox centre, the target man, is predictable and poses fewer problems, though Derek Johnstone, when he was with Rangers, was difficult because he was so good in the air.

Sturrock's movement off the ball is exceptional. He hasn't been a prolific scorer for Dundee United but he is excellent at drawing defenders into false areas for the benefit of his team. McGhee at Aberdeen played off the cuff. Nobody knew what he was going to do — I suspect this included Mark himself — and this made it a thankless task for defenders trying to dominate him. Goals frequently appear to come off him luckily but it happens too often to be accidental. He's a bit like Preben Elkjaer of Denmark who played against us in the World Cup.

Willie Miller, Alex McLeish and Jim Leighton have been

CR SMITH

Aberdeen's backbone for many years. At one time they were easily the most outstanding defensive trio in the country. Not now, though, with the advent of Butcher and company at Ibrox. And, of course, there's still Paul Hegarty and David Narey at Tannadice.

Just a few years ago Aberdeen were the best team in the country but then they also had Gordon Strachan, McGhee and Eric Black. They were also an annoying side. Alex Ferguson wound them up so well that I felt they were trying to run Scottish football and were getting away with a lot in the process.

I was surprised that Neale Cooper went to Aston Villa. It seemed he was being groomed to take a key role at Pittodrie for the future. At one point he very nearly joined Celtic but, instead, signed a short-term contract with the Dons.

Willie Miller is a 100 per center. Maybe he is starting to lose a wee bit of pace but he offsets this with his tremendous experience and outright determination in the role of sweeper — in one of the few teams in Scotland playing to this style. Miller, like me, could probably have gone to England earlier in his career but I am certain he now feels the challenge of the Premier League is as healthy as can be found anywhere.

I will be happy to play out my career with Celtic. Truthfully, there is no other team for me and I can't imagine having the privilege of playing in front of such great supporters with any other club. The bonus for me is that Celtic are the club I've supported since I was a boy. Players are not always lucky enough to be signed by their favourite team. For me, though, Parkhead is a "Bear's Paradise"! I simply can't imagine wearing any other jersey and, anyway, my contract doesn't expire until 1989. Hopefully, I'll have a few years after that.

It's a pity Scotland lost a character like Gordon Strachan but Manchester United are a really big club and I know he is very happy there. I don't think the Dons — and I am not trying to be superior here — rate in overall success with the Old Firm, Manchester United or Liverpool. However, if Manchester United had approached me I'm pretty sure I would have become a rarity by being one of the few ever to say "no" to them. That's how happy and grateful I am to be at Parkhead.

Looking back on some of the marvellous games we've had against Rangers, players who stand out in my mind are John Greig and Alex

MacDonald, now manager of Hearts. MacDonald riled me on the park but he was a smashing player for Rangers. Alex chirped away during games and sometimes jumped in late to tackle. All to get the opposition going. Although he was an annoying wee player I respected him. What a job he did at Ibrox.

John Greig was a superb Rangers man. I remember playing Rangers on my 18th birthday — 24 November 1977 — and Bobby Lennox broke his ankle. We won with a Joe Craig goal in 36 minutes but the incident leading up to Bobby's mishap overshadowed the victory. Kenny Dalglish and I were involved in the goal but we were all much more concerned about my very good mate Bobby. Greig brought Bobby down and it was in the tackle that he was injured. The referee at first gave a penalty but — a rare event — changed his mind after talking to a linesman.

Next day Greig really showed the kind of man he is. Although he had taken a fair amount of stick about the challenge on Bobby he turned up unannounced at the Lennox home in Saltcoats to apologise to Bobby. This summed Greig up for me. He was, and still is, one the game's good guys. People have compared me to Greig as a player and this is a compliment. Like most of my team-mates I relished games against Greig but I always felt he was a man I would like to have on my side in club games.

By the way, Joe Craig had been signed only two months before this from Partick Thistle. That goal in front of 43,500 at Ibrox paid off a large chunk of his £60,000 transfer fee. Celtic had been going through a bad spell against Rangers and this was our first win since January 1974.

In the current Rangers side it's impossible not to be impressed by Terry Butcher. I played against him in the under-21s at Coventry when Scotland lost 2-1 — Terry is a month younger than me. I noticed right away his skill with his left foot and his composure, assets he has demonstrated with Rangers. It certainly didn't surprise me that he has done so well since being transferred from Ipswich for £750,000. He is also one of Bobby Robson's international stalwarts. The England manager clearly rates Butcher as the No. 1 centre-half in the south.

I played against Graham Roberts when he was with Spurs. He is a great competitor and that is a major factor in his success. Attitude is first and foremost with me. It's vital to approach playing and training in the right way to be consistently successful. The will to win

Graham Roberts and Mo Johnston chase the ball.

is the base on which skill can be maximised. Roberts has ability but, having been suspended 13 times in England, a reputation which wasn't totally fair preceded him to Ibrox. He was red-carded in a match against Hamilton and, from what I saw on TV, he certainly looked unfortunate.

Goalie Chris Woods has played very well against Celtic. He is top-class and I would say it will not be long before he takes over from Peter Shilton in the England goal on a permanent basis. Woods made two memorable saves when Rangers beat Celtic 2-0 on New Year's Day 1987. One was from Paul McStay and another from Brian McClair which he put round a post.

Graeme Souness himself seems to be revelling as player-manager at Ibrox. It's as if he was conducting an orchestra in every match. I fancy being a manager eventually myself — although this is a long way into the future — so I am interested in how Graeme progresses in this area.

Over the years Ally McCoist has scored a lot of goals for Rangers. He's always been difficult against us. Ibrox fans give him stick at times but I feel this isn't justified. McCoist works hard and snatches goals. That's what he's meant to do.

On his game Davie Cooper is as good as or better than most. No Scottish winger has more skill. Over the past couple of seasons he has been a lot more consistent. He has had a new lease of life under Graeme Souness and Walter Smith.They have brought out the best in him.

John McClelland's departure to Watford was a surprise. He is a reliable player and was a good captain at Ibrox. But before anybody gets the mistaken idea that I've joined the Rangers Supporters' Club let me make it clear the three top men in my football life are Kenny Dalglish, Danny McGrain and Bobby Lennox. More of them after I instance the difficulties of being an Old Firm player by citing the cases of Iain Ferguson and Cammy Fraser.

Ferguson and Fraser were excellent with Dundee and that's why Jock Wallace signed them. Ferguson is carrying on the good work with Dundee United, having moved there when it became clear things weren't working out at Ibrox. However, playing for provincial clubs — this is not said snootily — is vastly different. Good performances are highlighted and mistakes largely ignored because players are expected to make them. With Celtic or Rangers the position is reversed. Any error is played up and the good things are taken more or less for granted. I believe this is right. Genuine success comes from ensuring that, where possible, mistakes are made only once or not at all. Celtic and Rangers men must perform well every single week of the year. If they don't they're out. With smaller clubs players get away with mediocre games much more easily than at Parkhead or Ibrox. Our fans demand success. They simply will not tolerate failure.

I don't have sleepless nights — well, not often — worrying about games. But I do get concerned from time to time. The fans are good to me. I think they know I would never ever pull on a Celtic or Scotland jersey without giving maximum effort.

Over the years I have felt it's just as well Alan Rough isn't the sensitive type. With Partick Thistle, Hibs and Scotland the amiable goalie has taken more than a fair share of criticism. He's had some super matches against Celtic and I've been in Scotland teams when he was outstanding. Laid-back though he may be, Roughie is an uncompromising type. The game that summed up his character best was when he came on as a second-half sub for Jim Leighton in the international against Wales which Scotland needed to draw at least to get to Mexico. He was brilliant and had a major influence on the Scotland team because of the composed way he handled himself. Very few goalkeepers could have come on in such a key match and performed so well.

Roughie is a class guy. I must also mention here Hamish McAlpine who was a staunch member of Dundee United's championship-winning side in season 1982-83. His clearances were like guided missiles.

The Motherwell pairing I recall most were Willie Pettigrew and Bobby Graham. They had a tremendous understanding. Sometimes, though, excellent players can be missed by the bigger clubs. One such example was Gerry McCabe when he was at Clydebank. His midfield play was superb and he was always on the ball and aware of people around him. I was surprised a big club didn't have a go for him before he went to Hamilton.

Now to the trio whose worth I can speak about best of all as I played with each of them. When I first went into the Celtic team Danny McGrain was the best right-back in Britain, maybe even the world. He was the most consistent player I've known. Week in, week out Danny was simply superb. He is great at cutting out crossfield passes — the ones from right-half to outside-left, I mean. What baffled me was that opposing clubs didn't realise it was hopeless to attempt such a pass with McGrain in opposition. In addition Danny set up so many chances he was really a full-back and winger all in one.

When Danny went down in a challenge he reacted like a rubber ball. On his feet immediately and on with the game. Without doubt he is the most amazing athlete of my time. Who would suspect, if they didn't know his remarkable background, that he has overcome problems such as a fractured skull, rheumatoid arthritis, a serious ankle injury and diabetes? His skull healed, the arthritis cleared up after acupuncture treatment, the ankle was cured after a long lay-off and the diabetes is now controlled by insulin injections.

Danny, I know, has been a tremendous example and inspiration to diabetics, particularly youngsters, who see by his example that life can still go on for them. I remember Danny put on weight tremendously when he was off because of his ankle. He was as broad as he was tall. Well, nearly! He really knocked his pan in to get fit. The abiding memory of Danny will be that he was truly an outstanding professional.

I'm also proud to have played with Bobby Lennox. He was a first-class professional and has the same approach now to his coaching work at Parkhead. He taught me a great deal about the importance of training and being in bed early. He is the type who is so dedicated that he can train purposefully on his own. This is harder than you may think. Training in a group is one thing but when your only companion is a dog it's a bit different. Bobby used to go out on the roads at home regularly, and particularly in the close season. Quite rightly, Bobby believed that fitness is all-important for a successful player. He passed this on to me.

Bobby went to play in Houston, Texas, when he thought his career was over with Celtic but it is a mark of the man's ability that Billy McNeill brought him back to Parkhead.

I have also been fortunate to play with lads like Charlie Nicholas — what skills he has! — Paul McStay, Tommy Burns and Davie Provan, who sadly has been affected by illness. The most artistic of all my present or former clubmates, though, was Kenny Dalglish. He had so much ability he could change a game — as, indeed, he is still doing at Liverpool where is now player-manager. Kenny was appointed to succeed Joe Fagan the day after the 1-0 defeat by Juventus in the European Cup final in Brussels which will always be remembered because of the tragedy in which 39 fans died. He has been so successful as a team boss since that he seemed to trigger off a new fashion of appointing player team bosses.

Oddly enough, when I first came into the team Kenny was getting stick from the fans. Imagine that! I think the supporters expected too much from him in *every* game. Before he went south I had two full seasons in the same team as Kenny and, of course, we've played

Referee Bob Valentine in the midst of protesters.

together for Scotland. Kenny and Danny had a splendid understanding. For instance, at a throw-in Kenny would allow the ball to go past him, knowing precisely how Danny would give it to him, and then swivel and as often as not have a shot at the target. His reading of play is uncanny and the way he shields the ball from defenders with his body is brilliant. A defender making the mistake of going too close to Kenny will find he is round him in a flash. While at Parkhead Kenny won four championship medals, four Scottish Cup winners medals and one in the League Cup.

Charlie Nicholas comes close to Kenny for skill but, of course, has not had nearly the same success. At Parkhead, he had an ideal partner in Frank McGarvey, who did a lot of the grafting. I believe that Charlie hasn't done as well as expected in England because he doesn't get enough of the ball. Our style at Parkhead is to get the ball up the park and, when Charlie was there, to land it at his feet. Nicholas is good at turning opponents. He is a master at having the ball at his feet and his back to an opponent — and then stepping over the ball to face a surprised defender. He is so quick at getting round it is astonishing.

It's hard to say whether or not Charlie left Celtic too quickly.

What I will say is that 50 goals a season went with him to Highbury. I believe he simply got an offer he couldn't possibly refuse. Arsenal's gain was Celtic's great loss.

Do I hear angry shouts from Edinburgh? I haven't forgotten Hearts, who probably have as good a side as they've ever had. Their strength is the front three of Sandy Clark, John Robertson and John Colquhoun, who are all hard workers and difficult to oppose. There's no pussyfooting. The system is to get the ball up to them as quickly as possible.

Clark is a real handful. He is a very honest player but I do think referees let him away with quite a lot. Sandy jumps into people but always gets on with the game. He takes a battering himself because of the way he throws himself about but he never protests. Players overacting infuriate me. Clark would never come into this category. He is a competitor — the kind I like on my side.

The Players' Union have rightly condemned swallow-divers who try to get fellow professionals into trouble. I detest this. Nothing to do with Sandy, either, but another new tactic creeping into the game is the elbow from the front. When forwards jump they are throwing their hands up as well and catching defenders on the face.

It would suprise me if my old rival Sandy Jardine didn't agree about this. I've played against him when he was at Ibrox and now Tynecastle and he is one of Scotland's all-time greats. Did Rangers release him too soon? Not for me to say but he has certainly done a wonderful job for Hearts who have also appointed him co-manager. Sandy is another player who has looked after his fitness carefully and is reaping the rewards.

The upward swing in the fortunes of Scottish football is very encouraging. I would like to see only full-time teams in a Premier League of ten clubs. I realise the costs which would be involved for clubs but if they want to operate in the big-time they should aim at certain standards.

Once a one up, one down situation is achieved it will be better for clubs who want to invest in themselves. The risk of demotion will be halved. This has been a worry for enterprising clubs. They could embark on ambitious plans and see them wrecked only a year later by being relegated. Forty-four league games in a season is also too many and that's what a 12-club League means. It's asking a lot of the players and the customers who have only a limited amount of money to spend on football.

The three smart gents at a charity dinner are Bobby Lennox, Roy and former boxing champion Jim Watt.

What the Premier League has provided is a competition which is as tight as there is anywhere in the world. A couple of defeats and teams can slip out of the running. Competition for the title is harder than it has ever been.

Another bonus for fans who believe there is life outside Parkhead and Ibrox is that Old Firm dominance doesn't exist any more. People argue that standards have slipped and this has allowed Aberdeen, Dundee United and to a lesser extent Hearts to come on. I disagree. These teams have sharpened up and the Premier League is surely more of a tactical league than the old First Division ever was. Teams have become increasingly difficult to break down. This is because they have managers who are planning ahead and laying out a sound match plan designed to give the opposition the least possible chance. Breaking down defences is more and more difficult. They are all well organised.

Ability-wise the Premier League is on a par with the First Division in England. It's nonsense to say competition or talent is any better in the south. That's why Richard Gough could leave Dundee United in a £750,000 transfer deal and slot in so well with Tottenham that manager David Pleat quickly made him his team captain. Celtic, Rangers, Aberdeen, Dundee United and Hearts would certainly give a good account of themselves against any opposition from England. The only reason Terry Butcher and his mates were surprised to find the quality so high in Scotland was the one I've already mentioned — lack of TV projection south of the border.

The other big bonus for us is the chance of playing in Europe. The top men in the south really miss this because of the UEFA ban on English clubs following the tragedy at the Heysel Stadium. European football brings in much-needed revenue but, more important, it prevents players and managers becoming insular. Wider standards are offered for comparison.

A snag about the Premier League, though, is the fact that we meet each other four times each season. Because of this we get to know each other pretty well. Some of the excitement goes out of matches. Familiarity is something we could do without but I suppose it's inevitable. So European football becomes even more stimulating. We meet and try to combat players whom we may only have read about in football magazines. Success in Europe is something which also keeps up the interest of the fans. They want variety as much as the players. Friendlies can relieve the pressure of the League but they are not a substitute for the real thing in any of the three major European competitions.

A lot of things are changing in football and moves could be more rapid than we imagine. Artificial pitches — Stirling Albion are Scotland's experimenting club — could become popular and maybe even profitable to clubs. Grounds are likely to be utilised more and more as recreation centres. It will all be intended to bring in more cash as costs go up every year.

There is certainly no need for gloom and doom. The game in Scotland is in safe hands and I feel it can only get even better.

Two of the most determined players in the game — Roy and Sandy Clark of Hearts. This was during Celtic's opening League game at Parkhead on 12 August 1987 and they won 1-0.

Chapter 12

REFEREEING IS THANKLESS

I WOULD hate to be a referee. They have a thankless job but I think that at £40 per match it is a hobby whereas for most Premier League players it is their livelihood. So I think referees should show more understanding — and, above all, consistency.

The referee I like most is cup final man Kenny Hope, from Clarkston. He comes over as a human being who seems to understand what footballers are about and that passion and the will to win are a large part of the competitors' make-up. Kenny is quite capable of replying to a heated protest by taking out his handkerchief and telling a player to dry his eyes. That kind of remark may be frowned on at the highest level, but I feel it breaks the tension and quite often can defuse a tricky situation.

One referee will let a player away with something and another penalise him. This can be infuriating. Referees, of course, are constantly being reminded by the SFA that they must clamp down on dissension, the tackle from behind and top players who try to run games. At one point I read that they were told they would be booted out if they didn't implement SFA instructions. Well, I can't blame the refs for doing what they are told. All I ask is that they are consistent because failure to be leads to confusion and irritation among players. And, perhaps, trouble.

Angrily kicking the ball way is another on the list of "dont's" in the clamp-down. Referees did stamp on this for a time but then relaxed. So players wonder what is going on — and some try to beat the system and may even get away with it.

I think the new plan of automatic suspension is better than the old idea of waiting for three or four weeks before being called before the SFA Disciplinary Committee. Now players serve their punishment a fortnight after picking up the penalty points or, for an ordering off, it's the next game or games. Points are calculated and dealt with over three years and this is why some players go on a two or even three-game automatic suspension. Basically there's a one-game ban for every ten points accumulated.

Defenders normally pick up five bookings a year. That's routine. But it also means that after three years on this total the minimum suspension is three games. It's a roll-on business. Five bookings means ten points and a one-game ban, 20 points means two, and 30 leads to three matches on the sidelines.

I suppose in fairness to referees every team feels a sense of injustice at some time. I always remember Davie Provan and Murdo MacLeod coming from Kilmarnock and Dumbarton. They thought a club like Celtic got every advantage from the match official. However, once they pulled on a Celtic jersey they were of the opinion that we got nothing.

I keep my distance from most referees because I feel that's the way they want it. Sometimes I feel meeting with refs to talk about the 17 laws of the game would be helpful. A ref with whom I'm quite friendly ran one of our matches in which the opposition employed delaying tactics. I pointed this out and he said he was watching and would add on time. When he blew for time up I thought he had forgotten what he had promised so I asked politely if I could see his watch. "Sure, Roy," he said. And when he looked at it with me he said: "Sorry . . . I forgot about the extra time." What could I say? I just shook my head and trooped off consoling myself that we all make mistakes.

A mistake among spectators, officials and players is to allow religion or any other factor to encroach on the game. When I'm seen at a function with Terry Butcher or any other Rangers players I hope it emphasises to people that we're not mortal enemies off the park. We can enjoy each other's company, doing things for charity and visiting fans in hospital. It would surprise you how many hospitals

The Skol Cup final and clearly Roy and teammates are not happy with referee Davie Syme's decision.

ask for Celtic and Rangers players to come together. We're delighted to do it.

When I hear "party" songs during games I often feel people singing them don't understand what they're really about. It should be football songs we hear rather than religious songs. If fans have those beliefs that's their affair, but I would much rather they kept them away from football. I play for Celtic because they are the football club I like most.

I think it is regrettable that religion should be a factor when evaluating footballers. This is not intended as a provocative statement. I believe this subject should be discussed openly and the more often this is done the better the chance of ridding ourselves of sectarian soccer.

Jock Stein was a Protestant and none could doubt my admiration for him. I'm not going to name them because religion is incidental to the game, but some great players with whom I've played were non Catholics, although it never occurred to me that this aspect of their lives was important — because in a football team it is most certainly shouldn't be. I will no doubt play alongside a lot more before my career ends. When scoring goals or saving them nobody, in my experience, stops to ask about religion. It's just daft.

I would like to think we are now approaching an age when football is an entertainment and the game is there to be enjoyed by everyone. Bigots are taboo. Support your team with all your heart but do so for the right reasons.

Alfie Conn is the only player in my time to have been with Rangers *and* Celtic. But he signed for us in March 1977, in a £65,000 deal with Tottenham. A couple of months later he played in the Celtic team that beat Rangers 1-0 in the Cup final. I don't remember Alfie looking sad to be the first to get a winners' medal with us as well as the other half of the Old Firm.

I read sometimes about footballers being prima donnas. I have seen no evidence of this. Certainly neither at Parkhead nor with Scotland are bigheads encouraged. They would cause friction and this is the last thing managers want. Every Celtic team I've played in has always contained down-to-earth lads and the atmosphere in the dressing-room has been good. I also think the attitude in Scottish dressing-rooms is better than it is over the border. I know players who've gone to England to find nobody would speak to them. This would never happen in Scotland. A new boy at Parkhead is immediately brought into things. It's part of my job as captain to make sure this happens but the lads do it without being told. It's called teamsmanship.

In a Scotland side all the lads mingle well and every step is taken to avoid cliques. People have said Charlie Nicholas is a prima donna. And Mo Johnston. And Graeme Souness. At some time or other this has been put about but in no way is any of it true. Perhaps stars like these three have an air of arrogance but it's arrogance in a good way. They are tops in their profession and I've never found them aloof. If such things were happening in a team at club or Scotland level the captain would be one of the men to tackle the problem. The fact that I've never had to do so merely confirms what I've said.

The captain's role in modern football does mean something more than just the honour although there's usually time to consult the bench if a tactical switch is required. I recollect what Billy McNeill told me about a captain's function. That is never to be seen to hang your head. If a skipper is playing badly himself he must see that this doesn't affect those around him.

Alan McInally powers the ball past a defender.

During a match I do a lot of shouting. But if I'm being critical it's never in any way to demean a colleague. It is intended to spur him on. Hopefully my shouts are constructive and get my mates motivated. I appreciate people shouting at me as well. If you make a mistake a helpful voice never goes wrong to get you back in the swing of things. In the Scotland side I may be playing with three or four other club team captains. Even so Andy Roxburgh has made it clear that when I'm Scotland captain I'm in charge on the park. Happily, I've never had to show my stripes!

There is still an important job for the team skipper to do but it's worth remembering that he has his own game to look after as well. However, it's not only being captain on the field that is important. We must handle ourselves well away from the pitch and also remember that good public relations is vital. If I go anywhere I have to keep in mind that I'm representing Celtic or Scotland. So do the other players but for the captain it's always that little bit more important.

All players feel a responsibility to the fans. At Parkhead our supporters have had a lot of success and they now expect more and more regularly. They are entitled to think this way. Players expect to win things as well. Successful people want to be with successful organisations and that's why I like being with Celtic. I think Celtic and Rangers are in the same category in this regard. If supporters are willing to stick by us week in, week out, we've got to give them something in return. We set our own standards and so do the fans. They expect at least one trophy every year.

If there's trouble in the crowd, players hate it. It's the last thing we want and especially among our own fans. I'm very happy to say that the behaviour of Celtic fans — indeed supporters throughout Scotland — has been good in recent years. And the spectators who follow the international side seem to keep out of bother commendably. Compared to some other countries Scots are "angels" but this is not to say we shouldn't be watching the situation carefully.

Behaviour of players when a goal is scored is always talked about. Nobody has ever tried to kiss me at any stage in a game and I most certainly couldn't see myself giving a team-mate a "cheeper". I do think that players in Britain are quite restrained in their jubilation after a goal. Nothing like the Brazilians, for instance. They go crazy. I don't see anything wrong, though, with players congratulating each other when a goal is scored. This is what they've been sweating

Roy with the Scottish Cup . . . in Celtic ribbons.

to achieve and it would seem a bit unnatural if they didn't show pleasure when it was achieved. However, I don't believe in going too far. Kissing is definitely out for me! I think the fans quite like it when the players hug and backslap after a goal. Usually they are doing something similar on the terracings and in the stand. It is a healthy sign to be elated when a target has been reached. I see nothing wrong in demonstrating this. In fact it would be pretty boring if players didn't react to a goal.

A lot of work goes into scoring and winning. You should see the dressing-room at half-time. With Scotland, Andy Roxburgh insists on silence while he talks immediately we go in at the interval. Once he has said his piece we can all make our points, to him or to each other.

Sometimes the discussions at club level can be chaotic as we all try to say what's on our mind. However, a manager can often earn his money — and the team a victory — by the tactical changes he may make or the players he gees-up by what he says. The most recurring advice to a team leading after the first half is to watch not to lose a goal just after half-time and undo the good work of the first 45 minutes. Some managers will tell a player he has ten minutes in the second half to assert himself — or be taken off. This is to make the player try harder. Usually it works. Nowadays substitutes warm up very nearly for 90 minutes if they aren't required to play. But not so long ago they just sat on the bench and the manager would tell one to warm up as a warning to the players on the pitch.

I've heard stories about rows in dressing-rooms during half-time but I've never witnessed anything like this myself. However, the importance of managers and their skills really comes to life in crucial games where changes have to be made — either to maintain command or gain it. Coaching is important. That's why I am an enthusiastic attender at the SFA summer coaching at Largs which I feel helps me as a player and will be invaluable when I move into coaching or management — if I'm lucky! — after I stop playing.

Chapter 13

CELTIC'S CONSISTENCY

IT is often said outside Parkhead that an essential part of a Celtic man's equipment is a chip for his shoulder. That's not true, of course. And I hope no one will think what I now say fuels this argument.

Do you realise that since Jock Stein first propelled Celtic to the top nine times in a row from season 1965-66 Celtic have been out of the top two places only twice — third in 1974-75 and fifth in 1977-78? This is a record in consistency which no other side in the Premier League can match but we haven't really been given much credit for it. The pressure is always on us to be first and, in this respect, the heyday times under Jock Stein may be rebounding on us. Celtic fans want only to win. Second prizes are not on the menu. They dine out on success.

However, we can't be tops all the time. Look at great clubs such as Real Madrid, Benfica and, nearer home, Manchester United. They have had great runs of success and then gone into a period of decline. I certainly don't think anybody could argue Celtic have been on a downswing for long and I say this in spite of the most recent disappointments which our supporters have had to endure.

I have five championship medals but the total should really have been seven . . . even eight had we performed consistently in 1986. We threw the title at Aberdeen in 1979-80 after being eight points clear at the beginning of March. Points were stupidly dropped and this included a run of seven draws in nine games.

In 1982-83 we were pipped by a single point by Dundee United who won the Premier League championship for the first time. Celtic were in front for almost all of the season but defeats by United and Aberdeen left us in the position of requiring the Tannadice side to lose a match — which they didn't. All the same, United were worthy champions and they clinched the flag by winning at Dens Park, which made it especially good for them. At the same time Celtic beat Rangers 4-2 at Ibrox — our seventh point out of the four games with them — and Charlie Nicholas left for Arsenal after scoring 29 League goals. But United's victory underlined the fierce challenge emerging from the north-east as well as the good management techniques of Jim McLean.

In 1986-87, of course, our title chance went when John Clark levelled the score at 1-1 in our game at Parkhead against, ironically, Dundee United. With three games to go we had to watch Rangers riding off into the sunset with the trophy every club wants most and which we came to regard as our own in the Stein era. Yet midway through the League we looked virtual certainties to win it.

I find it odd that I have only one League Cup winners' medal and that this was obtained in the season of United's triumph. It rounded off Billy McNeill's first Celtic managerial record very nicely — three Premier League flags and a triumph in the Scottish Cup and League Cup in the space of five years.

Nicholas put us on the road to victory in the League Cup final of December 1982 with a goal in 22 minutes. The move began from a throw-in by Danny McGrain. Davie Provan then had a run and made a good pass inside to Charlie who squeezed the ball inside Jim Stewart's left-hand post. Our second goal by Murdo MacLeod nine minutes later stemmed from a Provan corner. The ball was headed back from the far post by Tom McAdam and then bounced between me and Murdo. He shouted and I drew out of the way. Murdo rocketed the ball into the net from the edge of the penalty area. So at half-time Celtic were 2-0 up and Provan was having a superb game. In fact, he was deservedly named Man of the Match and won a holiday in Florida. A minute after half-time Jim Bett hit back. From 20 yards he slammed in a free kick after Tom McAdam had fouled Gordon Smith. However, Celtic held out and it was a win which pleased me a lot.

The critics didn't think it was a very good game and they included Tommy Gemmell. But it was my first League Cup winners' medal, so I found it difficult to agree! Tommy made the point that an injury to Paul McStay, then only 18, had upset Celtic's rhythm as he was playing so well and was so dominating in the midfield. This was true. He was off for the last 27 minutes of the final seen by 55,372 at Hampden Park. Gemmell was quoted as saying: "I thought McStay was Celtic's best player but not far behind came big Roy Aitken who had two vital interceptions late in the game." A nice compliment to both of us from Big Tam but I didn't disagree with the Press selection of Davie Provan.

Bobby Shearer calculated that it took Rangers 41 minutes to engineer a shot at our goal. He said that only Bobby Russell had looked the part "while Celtic had a handful of players who were in good form". I quote the teams to illustrate how quickly Old Firm sides change — *Celtic:* Bonner, McGrain, Sinclair, Aitken, McAdam, MacLeod, Provan, McStay (Reid), McGarvey, Burns, Nicholas. *Rangers*: Stewart, McKinnon, Redford, McClelland, Paterson, Bett, Cooper, Prytz (Dawson), Johnstone, Russell (MacDonald), Smith.

Rangers had obtained Gordon Smith on loan from Brighton and John Greig gambled desperately in fielding him. The move didn't really come off. It was simply too much to expect a player to come out of Brighton reserves to excel in a final such as this. Anyway, it was Celtic's ninth League Cup success and our 17th final in the competition. In 11 matches on the road to victory Celtic, remarkably, scored 41 goals.

I have four losers' medals in the League Cup. I am not boasting about this, of course. But I don't understand why our record is so ordinary because we have been to so many finals in this tournament. One of my biggest let-downs was losing 3-2 to Rangers in a semi-final which deprived us of being in our 15th final in a row. Mind you, this particular defeat happened on 13 December, 1978, so perhaps our bad luck was explicable, although I am not really superstitious.

Johnny Doyle had a particularly good game. He scored first, then Sandy Jardine levelled from a penalty. Davie Cooper had gone down after a challenge by Johannes Edvaldsson. There were a lot of protests and Tommy Burns was sent off by referee Hugh Alexander. This was balanced soon after half-time when Alex Miller received his marching orders for his second cardable tackle on Doyle. "Doylie" gave me a chance to score a second goal in 65 minutes but

Brian McClair is held aloft by Peter Grant after scoring against Rangers. Murdo MacLeod and Alan McInally are jubilant but Dave McPherson, now Hearts, is downcast.

big Peter McCloy managed to parry my shot. The ball went to Tom McAdam, however, and he scored easily. Colin Jackson brought Rangers back into the hunt in 80 minutes and then we went into the fateful extra-time.

That was a tragedy for Jim Casey who came on as a sub to replace Mike Conroy. In 113 minutes — note the time! — the ball bounced off the unlucky Casey's leg and rolled past Roy Baines. Poor Jim simply couldn't get out of the way of a mishit shot. And so Celtic lost and Rangers went on to beat Aberdeen 2-1 in the final.

Rangers certainly jinxed us that day — just as they did in the Skol League Cup final on 22 October 1986. Davie Hay was so incensed by our 2-1 defeat that he said acidly that Celtic should join the English League. No such thing was ever seriously mooted, however. It was Graeme Souness's first major trophy win and he was generous enough to say at the end that Celtic were the better team. Souness, by the way, was injured and was unable to play and we were minus the skills of Tommy Burns who was also under treatment at the time.

The game ended in mayhem after Davie Cooper scored an 84th minute penalty which some papers reported as being "very debatably awarded". Defeat was a tremendous disappointment for us as we had battled back after being 1-0 down to an Ian Durrant goal. Brian McClair was our scorer in 70 minutes and it was one of the best goals seen at Hampden in a decade.

Sadly, trouble overshadowed the play. Mo Johnston was sent off by referee David Syme and Stuart Munro was yellow-carded. A linesman spotted an off-the-ball incident while Rangers' Ally McCoist was being booked after receiving treatment. Syme called Johnston and Munro to the side, checked they were the right pair and then had to send Mo off because he had already been cautioned.

The final aggravation for us was that in the jostling which went on as Johnston was being sent off Tony Shepherd was also red-carded. During the stoppage Syme spoke to Shepherd and, as the referee turned to walk away, he felt a blow on the back of his head. His immediate — and wrong — conclusion was that Shepherd was the culprit. Out came the red card again and a bewildered Shepherd began to move off. However, thankfully, a linesman drew the referee's attention to a coin lying on the pitch. He also said Shepherd had done nothing. The coin had been thrown from the crowd.

So, before the match was restarted Tony was told a mistake had been made and he could continue with the game. He became the first player ever to be sent off in a Hampden final without missing a second of play. It was one of the most extraordinary things I have ever seen on a football field. I still wonder what would have happened had the game gone on without Shepherd and then it had been proved at the finish that the sending off was a mistake.

It was a sad Sunday for us. Indiscipline is not Celtic's style but we got carried away in what we thought was injustice. Remember, too, that we are a cavalier side prepared to take risks at the back because we believe in adventurous football. With this kind of attitude it makes it all the more perplexing when a referee appears to make a misjudgement.

I don't want to say too much about the penalty except that the jersey pulling between Terry Butcher and myself was very much two-way. Terry probably wouldn't have said anything if the foul had been given the other way. To be honest, I lost the ball and when I tried to go where I thought it was I stretched out my arm and Terry went down like a ton of bricks with me on top of him.

Terry is six feet four inches. There was no way I would beat him in a straight jump for the ball. We had been jostling with each other throughout the match as I was told to pick him up when he came forward. Don't read this as the carping of a poor loser — although I hate being on the wrong end of a score. — but several reasonable judges considered a penalty award was harsh. It is certainly not easy to lose such an important final in this fashion and I feel sure Rangers would have been similarly minded had they been in the same position.

The penalty decision was like one on the chin from Mike Tyson in the last round of a 15-rounder for the heavyweight title. I also feel that this victory gave Rangers a lift for the rest of the season — except, of course, when they played Hamilton Accies in the Scottish Cup!

The year before we were beaten in the quarter-final stage of the Skol Cup at Easter Road where we were level 2-2 with Hibs at half-time and 4-4 at full-time.

Four months before, a deal that would have taken Danny McGrain to Airdrie as player-manager fell down. Happily, Danny was given a new contract by Celtic and the club certainly never regretted it. However, in this particular tie with Hibs Danny had the misfortune to score for the opposition. And it was a 101st-minute goal which levelled one I had scored a minute before. So at 4-4 we

This is the controversial penalty incident involving Roy and Terry Butcher.

had to go into a penalty shoot-out. We lost 4-3. It was a smashing result for Hibs but in the final they lost 3-0 to Aberdeen and the Edinburgh team were disappointing.

I like to see two strong teams in Edinburgh, by the way. A powerful Hibs is important to Hearts. They thrive on the local competition just as the Old Firm get a spin-off from each other. It's the same with Dundee and Dundee United. Ideally, derbies should be unpredictable because of the current form of the teams.

That season illustrated the ups and downs a team can have. Hibs also defeated us 4-3 in the quarter-final of the Scottish Cup after we had led 1-0 at half-time. Yet only two months before this we had felt so good after beating Rangers 2-0 in the 100th League meeting between the two clubs. It was a milestone match and at Parkhead we think history is important in the game. Paul McGugan and Brian McClair scored in the first half and both were from headers.

Celtic's worst performance in the League Cup in my time — and I feel it is fair to mention this — was failing to qualify from our section in 1981-82. We were a point behind St Mirren with St Johnstone and Hibs below us. That was the season Rangers beat Dundee United 2-1 in the final.

For the record my losers' medals in League Cup finals were against Aberdeen and Rangers three times. That last statistic does tend to upset me. I intend, of course, to adjust this in the coming years.

Chapter 14

CHALLENGE OF EUROPE

THE fact that Scottish clubs are in Europe while the big guns from England are banned riles Bryan Robson and the other stars from south of the border. Euro football is vital but England's players are banished through no fault of their own. The bad behaviour of fans, following the Heysel Stadium tragedy in which 39 died, has caused it. The fact that other countries like Holland have had bad crowd scenes since then has not helped England's case in any way. UEFA, the governing European body, take the view that two wrongs don't make a right.

Danger of trouble among spectators is always present but I praise the followers, not only of Celtic, but every other Scottish club as well. They are discouraged from travelling, of course, by the SFA and I feel this is wise. However, I understand what urges fans who have followed a team through thick and thin to disregard this advice.

From a playing point of view the challenge of Europe cannot be bettered. It infuriates me that in my time at Parkhead we have never managed to get past the quarter-final stage in any of the three major tournaments.

The season after my quarter-final Cup Winners Cup debut against Sachsenring Zwickau, of East Germany, we met Wisla Krakow, of Poland. After drawing 2-2 we went down 2-0 in the away leg. World Cup striker Kmiecik scored twice just after half-time and ensured our exit in the first round. I almost managed to help with a fight-back goal. Paul Wilson took my pass which put him in the clear six yards out. He walloped the ball first time but 'keeper Gonet blocked it and the rebound went past off a post. The line-ups were — *Home:* Latchford, McGrain, Lynch, Glavin, MacDonald, Edvaldsson, Doyle, Dalglish, Wilson, Burns, Lennox. *Away:* Latchford, McGrain, Lynch, Pat McCluskey, Edvaldsson, MacDonald, Glavin, Aitken, Doyle (Lennox), Dalglish, Wilson. Only John Doyle appeared in the first team more often than me in that season so I felt I was making progress.

This was my second visit behind the Iron Curtain while still only a lad and it made me realise that Scotland has a lot of plus points no matter what we may say about the weather. The people of Poland have a tough time. I saw food queues and there is a lot of double-dealing in a money black market which goes on right under the noses of the authorities. It doesn't speak very highly of the country's economy. I would prefer always to be on this side of the Iron Curtain despite the relaxations now being introduced by Russia's leader, Mikhail Gorbachev.

In season 1977-78 we had our easiest passage ever in a European Cup tie, against Juenesse d'Esch of Luxembourg. Celtic won 5-0 at Parkhead and then 6-1 away. Ronnie Glavin and Johannes Edvaldsson scored a couple apiece in Luxembourg. The teams — *Home:* Latchford, McGrain, Lynch, Edvaldsson, MacDonald, McWilliams, Doyle (Lennox), Glavin (McLaughlin), Craig, Aitken, Wilson. *Away:* Latchford, McGrain, Kay, Casey (McLaughlin), MacDonald, Aitken, Glavin, Wilson, Craig (John McCluskey), Burns, Lennox.

In the second round, after winning 2-1 at home with goals by Joe Craig and Tommy Burns, there were again several injury problems for the return leg with SWW Innsbruck, of Austria. As in the home match I had to play right-back in place of Danny McGrain. In fact, Danny missed all but the first seven matches and Pat Stanton was so badly hurt in an opening league match that he eventually had to retire. It was a shame for the former Hibs star and the injury also cost Danny a place in Scotland's World Cup party in Argentina.

Innsbruck had spectator trouble around the time of our second-leg meeting in November 1977, so a switch was made to Salzburg which is one of the most picturesque places we've visited, a lovely town with countryside to match. No wonder it was picked for the filming of Julie Andrews' *The Sound of Music*. I might mention here that I no longer play the piano, as many of my Press friends appear to think. I got a diploma from the London School of Music but that was when I was 15 and, sadly, I gave up then.

Back to football. The game was awful. Not for the first or the last time relations between a Scottish and Austrian club were strained. Andy Lynch was sent off ten minutes from the end for allegedly punching an opponent. It was a thoroughly nasty 90 minutes with a lot of crude tackles. Why this should happen between Scots and Austrians is inexplicable. But hostility does seem to exist and at international level as well. All we wanted to do afterwards was get home as quickly as possible. The teams — *Home:* Latchford, Aitken, Lynch, Edvaldsson, MacDonald, Casey, Doyle, Glavin, Craig, Burns, Wilson (Conn, Lennox). *Away:* Latchford, Aitken, Lynch, Glavin, MacDonald, Casey, Doyle, Edvaldsson, Craig, Burns, Wilson. We were out of Europe again after a 2-1 victory for us at Parkhead was followed by a 3-0 loss away.

Having finished a miserable fifth in the League next season we had to make do with the Anglo-Scottish Cup, a competition which wasn't really a success because leading English clubs didn't take it seriously. Celtic dismissed Clyde by an 8-2 aggregate score and failed 3-1 over two games against Burnley. The matches were a poor substitute for Europe.

My most exciting season in the European Cup was 1979-80. In the first round we had to go off into unknown territory in Albania. The régime was so testy the Press weren't allowed to accompany us. This had not happened before and certainly has not since. Celtic made a protest to UEFA about the failure to give facilities to the reporters but it fell on deaf ears.

Since Albania had broken off diplomatic relations with all the major powers — and this included Britain — nobody knew anything about the country. Or very little at any rate. Chris White had to go to Paris to obtain visas from the Albanian Consul there. This was the nearest consulate to Glasgow. Information about Partizan Tirana was as scant as intelligence about the country. But Billy McNeill told us before the match that the 25,000 crowd would be quiet and respectful. I suspect Billy was guessing or just judging from what he had experienced in Eastern Bloc countries. Albanians are Communists but they don't want to know Russia or China.

From the kick-off the ball was driven down the left and pushed on by a wee winger who then smashed it across the face of the goal. Mike Conroy turned it out for a corner. Silence my foot! The ground erupted. The Albanians went off their rockers. They made the Parkhead Jungle sound quiet.

There was much more clamour to come, though. Out of nothing Comrade Murati won the game for Partizan ten minutes from the interval. A long ball came in from the left wing. The sun was high in the sky and blazing. When Peter Latchford jumped he lost the ball in the glare. It went over his head and Murati danced in at the far post and headed it home.

We felt unlucky not to have won but felt reasonably confident we would clinch the tie at Parkhead. Anyway, we were happy to be on the way home. The way of life in Albania seemed odd to us. When we arrived the streets were mobbed. The people seemed to have nothing else to do but talk and stare. When we went out for a stroll to the main square in Tirana people were walking around aimlessly. Men were hand-in-hand but this seemed to be the thing to do. Chatting to each other was the number one recreation. The people were friendly enough but their existence is so isolated they couldn't be blamed for appearing a bit suspicious of us. It was, after all, Communists meeting so-called Capitalists. I certainly won't be going there for my holidays, although it is just across the Mediterranean from Corfu.

The food was different, too. It was soup and chicken for three days. Only two of our party could take the soup — Roddie MacDonald and Bobby Lennox — but they would eat anything! The rest of us stuck to a diet of chicken which is much the same anywhere in the world.

In the return leg I scored from two headers and we won 4-1. But only after a freak start. A long ball from the Partizan defence hit off Alan Sneddon's head as big Peter came out to grab it. The ball spun into the net and we were 1-0 down after only 15 minutes. Partizan didn't have one supporter with them so the stunned silence at Parkhead has rarely been more emphatic. However, Roddie MacDonald levelled five minutes later and Vic Davidson got another sandwiched between my two. We were 4-1 up at half-time and this is how it finished. We went through on a 4-2 aggregate.

An astonishing 51,000 crowd turned up at Parkhead. I think the fans thought the Albanians had two heads. For my part I won't readily forget Albania and the "street-walkers" interested only in passing the time of day with each other. It could never happen on Sauchiehall Street. Teams — *Away:* Latchford, Sneddon, McGrain, Aitken, McAdam, Conroy, Provan, Davidson, McCluskey (Doyle), MacLeod, Lennox. *Home:* Latchford, Sneddon, McGrain, Aitken, MacDonald, McAdam, Provan, Davidson, McCluskey (Lennox), MacLeod, Doyle.

The second round took us to Dundalk in Ireland and I must say I've never felt under so much pressure. We didn't play well at Parkhead although winning 3-2. *Celtic:* Latchford, Sneddon, McGrain, Aitken, MacDonald, McAdam, Provan, Davidson, McCluskey (Lennox), MacLeod, Doyle.

Dundalk knew a 1-0 victory in the return would be good enough. We were jittery and certainly I've never seen Billy NcNeill so worried. The park was heavy and extra seating had been put into the packed stadium. The place was crammed. Dundalk had everything to gain and we had the lot to lose. It was the first time I experienced Celtic playing five across the back, which underlines just how jumpy we were.

Dundalk played a 4-4-2 with two big strikers whom MacDonald and McAdam were to mark with me in the role of spare man playing it safe behind them. The game finished a goalless draw. It was 90 minutes of anxiety and I recall just a minute from the end a ball coming over from the right. It went through a Dundalk forward's leg and he missed what could have been a certain goal. Had we lost it would have been the worst result in Celtic's history. Thank goodness we didn't. It was our Great Escape. The team that day — 9 November 1979 — was: Latchford, McGrain, Aitken, McAdam, MacDonald, MacLeod, Provan, Conroy, Edvaldsson, Lennox, Burns (Davidson).

And so to Real Madrid. Like Barcelona when they played Dundee United much more recently in the UEFA Cup, the mighty Spaniards were sprinkled with great names such as Del Bosque — one of the best I ever played against — Juanita, Santillana, Comacho, the West German Stielike and the Englishman Laurie Cunningham.

There was a crowd of 67,000 at Parkhead and Celtic were favourites — to lose. Billy McNeill tried desperately to play down Real's talents. "Don't bother about all these names in the Spanish team," he said to us only minutes before we went out. "They're nobodys really. Take Juanita. In Scottish that means wee Johnny. So what have you got to worry about from a man with a name like

Roy's on the ball but momentarily distracted.

that?" We knew what Billy was trying to do. He was adjusting facts and trying to give us the advantage of thinking we were playing against just another team. However, it is difficult to devalue known class in a few sentences.

It worked in the first game though. We won 2-0 with goals by George McCluskey (52 minutes) and Johnny Doyle (74 minutes). Celtic played as well that night as any side in which I've played. The second half was blistering. Goalie Garcia Ramon fumbled a low shot by Alan Sneddon. When the ball bounced from his body McCluskey blasted the ball into the net. I've rarely heard such loud cheering at Parkhead, known around Europe for its clamour. It sounded like music to the players. Sneddon was involved in the second half goal as well. He took a pass from Murdo MacLeod, whipped it to the far post and Doyle finished off with a header. None who played or watched will forget that game for which the team was: Latchford, Sneddon, McGrain, Aitken, McAdam, MacDonald, MacLeod, Provan, Lennox, McCluskey, Doyle.

The attendance at the famous Bernabeu Stadium in Madrid for the return was 110,000. It was a spectacular setting. I like watching old games on TV on my video at home. Each time I look I see new things. I've just been having a look at the Madrid game and we had some great chances in the first half. We could have sewn it up in the first 45 minutes but, instead, there was no scoring until a minute from the interval. By then we had hit the bar and missed a couple bang in front of goal. Real were certainly under pressure.

Almost on half-time our luck broke the wrong way, with some assistance for Real from the referee. He penalised Latchford for overcarrying. I couldn't believe it as he ordered a free-kick two yards inside the box. The ball went out for a corner and when the kick was taken big Peter went for it. I thought he was pushed as he did so. It spun free and bounced off Roddie MacDonald's leg to Santillana who poked it into goal. The crowd exploded with delight, except of course for the Celtic posse huddled together in the huge stand. They let us know they were there all right but hope now began to sink fast. Real's players were so overjoyed they clearly would have preferred to have no interval. They had the initiative and wanted to hold it.

When we came out in the second half we felt dejected but prepared to battle on. However, spurred by that unexpected goal Real ran over the top of us. It was the most disappointing end to a European tie which I have experienced. Stielike and Juanito got two more goals and that was us on the way home, beaten on a 3-2 aggregate. We had seemed so close to getting to the semi-finals until that refereeing break changed the course of the match. The team: Latchford, Sneddon, McAdam, MacDonald, McGrain, Provan, Aitken, Doyle, MacLeod, McCluskey (Burns), Lennox.

So my Euro dream ended again in misfortune. It has been the Celtic story in Europe ever since I joined the club, but more, lots more, drama was to follow.

At this point I should make it clear that on Euro trips we don't often go sightseeing. We are abroad to work. Hence the fact that although I've been in Madrid several times for games I don't know a lot about the city. It's an imposing place, a good deal bigger than Glasgow, but apart from shopping briefly for the family I haven't been around it very much. Our trips are becoming shorter. Often now if the club has chartered a plane we will leave soon after the game and be home around midnight. Years ago there were banquets for the players and officials but this has happily been abandoned.

Alan Sneddon played with us in Europe for the last time in the Cup Winners Cup. In January 1981, he left Celtic for Hibs and Pat Bonner also took over from Peter Latchford as our regular goalie. We beat Diosgyoeri of Hungary 6-0 at Parkhead with Frank McGarvey getting a hat-trick, George McCluskey two and Dom Sullivan the other one. The unusual thing was that all the goals came in the second half. This was our high-flying team: Bonner, Sneddon, McGrain, Aitken, McAdam, MacLeod (Doyle), Provan (Nicholas), Sullivan, McGarvey, Burns, McCluskey. In the return leg, which meant a long bus trip from Budapest, Celtic lost 2-1 after Charlie Nicholas put us ahead in 24 minutes. However, the result didn't matter a lot. Celts coasted through on a 7-2 aggregate. The only change in the team from the first leg was Nicholas in place of McCluskey.

Hungary, I can say, is pleasant. Surprisingly, it is run on the same economic lines as this country and is unlike a Communist régime. If a factory isn't paying then it is closed. This would delight Mrs Thatcher. In Budapest, the capital, there are big hotels like the Hilton which have backers from the West. It would be a nice place to visit since it gives the impression of being remote from the control of the Kremlin. In fact they say it is the Paris of the Eastern Bloc.

Our next game took us behind the Iron Curtain again but Romania is vastly different — a country of hard-line Reds with a way of life westerners wouldn't fancy. The second round opposition was provided by Politechnica Timisoara. In the home leg Celtic were vastly superior but only won 2-1. We should have gone to Romania nearly as safe as we were in the previous round. Unhappily, this was far from being the case. Charlie scored both goals at Parkhead. The first came when the Romanian 'keeper failed to hold a shot from Davie Provan and Nick nicked a goal as a result. Charlie doesn't mess about. He got the second three minutes from half-time, heading in a lob from Murdo MacLeod. We looked set for another big score but in the second half goals went out of fashion for us and the Romanians grabbed a crippling away counter when the ball bounced off Pat Bonner's hand into the goal. This proved decisive in the final reckoning.

We knew in our hearts we could be in big trouble in Romania but this turned out to be an understatement because of a Greek referee who was quite simply unbelievable. Roddie MacDonald was sent off with the home player Manea in just under 20 minutes. Roddie had tried to shoot as 'keeper Moise dived at his feet. Manea didn't like this and made the point forcibly. So it was red cards for both.

Then Timisoara snatched a 1-0 victory when Latchford was pushed as the ball came from the right. I didn't think the foul was in doubt but tried to scramble the ball away as a precaution. Unfortunately, striker Paltinisan got to it first and fired into goal. I thought my Greek friend was certain to disallow it. More fool me. He didn't — to the joy of the home crowd. Soon afterwards Frank McGarvey was sent off for arguing after previously being yellow-carded.

The referee was a joke — the worst I've seen. I think he was later banned over another game. John Clark, our assistant manager at the time, certainly found himself in trouble with UEFA over scathing remarks he was alleged to have made. John denied adamantly that he had opened his mouth but UEFA still banned him from European games for a couple of seasons. The Greek referee seemed to have done up Celtic in every direction.

Again it was a bad way to go out, on a 2-2 aggregate with the goal scored at Parkhead swinging the decision for Timisoara. This is the way in Europe. Teams can be lifted up and then dropped like a bag of cement. Teams — *Home:* Bonner, Sneddon, McGrain, Aitken, McAdam, MacLeod (Conroy), Provan (Doyle), Sullivan, McCluskey, Burns, Nicholas. *Away:* Latchford, Sneddon, McAdam,

MacDonald, McGrain, Sullivan, Aitken, MacLeod, McGarvey, Nicholas, Provan.

In 1981-82 Celtic romped to their 33rd league title after leading throughout the season. The highlight was our meeting with the star-studded Italian club Juventus in the first round of the European Cup. We found ourselves opposing, among others, half a dozen of the Italian team who were to win the World Cup in Spain — Gentile, Cabrini, Furino, Scirea, Tardelli and Bettega. On top of this there was that classy Republic of Ireland international midfielder Liam Brady who has now ended his sojourn in Italy and is playing with West Ham. Billy McNeill went to Turin to have a look at Juventus and he gave us a balanced warning about the calibre of the opposition.

It was my first sight of the superb 'keeper Dino Zoff in an opposing team. With a name like that, I thought, he should be in Frank Sinatra's rat-pack. Zoff was at that time 40 — 21 years older than Charlie Nicholas. I recall him as a big, amiable man and a really fine player. He actually took part in four World Cup finals — in Mexico, West Germany, Argentina and Spain — which is quite a record.

A crowd of 60,017 saw our first-leg tie at Parkhead. We were glad to have the first game at home as this would then put us in the position of knowing precisely what we had to do to qualify in Turin two weeks later. Danny McGrain shook off a heavy cold to captain us and this was the side which brought off a sensational 1-0 victory against the millionaire Italians: Bonner, McGrain, Reid, Aitken, McAdam, MacLeod, Provan, Sullivan, Nicholas, Burns, McCluskey. A spectacular goal by Murdo MacLeod put us in business for the second leg and really shook the Italians rigid. We certainly gave as good as we got but they were a team reserving themselves for what they were sure would be the kill second time around.

Charles Corver, the well-respected Dutch referee, turned down two reasonable Celtic penalty claims in that game. It was clear he wanted nothing to do with controversy and his way of avoiding it was to say "no" to everything. In one incident in which centre-back Brio brought down George McCluskey late in the match Corver actually ran towards the penalty spot and then seemed to change his mind and direction.

The goal by the maurauding MacLeod was scored in 65 minutes. We had been running ourselves into the ground with nothing to show for it. Then Davie Provan played for a corner and won it. From the corner flag he sent the ball swirling in towards the six-yard box where yours truly hit it on the volley. The shot was blocked. However, the ball careered towards Murdo who was running in at full tilt. He hit it dead on and Zoff scrambled to his right to grab it. Hard luck on him — it glanced off Scirea and shot off in the opposite direction to spin into the net. To say we were delighted is something of an understatement.

In the first half Celtic created chances — near things, you might say, but truthfully they didn't worry Zoff overmuch. Pat Bonner, on the other hand, had a particularly good save from Tardelli when Brady, whose passing and reading of the play were exceptional throughout, short-passed a free kick into his path. The goal was one of Murdo's most vital and highlighted his value as a marksman coming from the midfield. With Bonner he was Celtic's most used player that season with 46 appearances. He also scored 14 goals, including the one against Juventus. Murdo is a tenacious player and he was especially pleased when Jock Stein first picked him for Scotland.

When we went to Italy we stayed in wine-growing country at Asti. It was 60 kilometres from Turin but ensured us privacy from the hordes of Italian reporters and photographers. When it came to kick-off time, though, Juventus were given a rapturous reception at the Stadio Communale from a crowd of nearly 70,000, who had paid £226,000 — a lot of cash in these days, and it gives some idea how Italian clubs could pay so much more than British clubs to their stars.

However, during this second leg we found Juventus were completely different in attitude and deployment. Pat Bonner was in superb form and but for him we would have lost by more than 2-0. It was one of the best goalkeeping displays I have ever seen at any level. Our team was: Bonner, Moyes, Reid, Aitken, McAdam, MacLeod, Provan, Sullivan, McGarvey, Burns, McCluskey. Danny McGrain was injured so I was captain and Davie Moyes took over the right-back role. What a Euro baptism at 19. We missed Danny's experience but Davie had a good match.

It would be churlish not to admit that the better team won. They were so experienced and knew more about the requirements at this level than we did. Celtic were basically a young team. It was outright optimism for us to have imagined we could KO them over two legs. It was a David against Goliath contest.

Roy Aitken, a player with plenty to laugh about.

They played entirely different styles in the two legs. At Parkhead they were on the defensive and this is what kidded us that we had a good chance after winning the opener. In Turin they gave us a lesson in the art of the fast break-out. They were simply electric. Brady was again immaculate despite a muscle injury which almost kept him out of the game. He was the schemer-in-chief.

Just before half-time Brady nearly knocked Bonner off his feet by the sheer power of a 20-yard shot. Pat blocked it, one of several splendid saves he made. We had been composed until we had lost a 28th-minute goal scored by Virdis. When the fiery little skipper Furino drove the ball quickly upfield, Marocchino passed it to the even then greying Bettega and his ball to Virdis was so good Bonner from then on had no chance. None of us managed even to touch the ball from the time the move started.It was all up hill after that.

Five minutes from the interval Virdis made trouble for us again. He picked up the ball from a free kick and swept it to Bettega who swivelled and shot home with his left foot. The pace slackened in the second half but hard as we tried we couldn't get a goal against such a fine defence. So Juventus went through on a 2-1 aggregate. Although the *Daily Record* described Alex Ponnet, the Belgian referee, as acting "like a newly recruited member of the Juventus fan club", and although it was Celtic Football Club's 100th European tie, this game demonstrated to us the meaning of genuine class. I wasn't at all surprised when Italy won the World Cup in Spain less than a year later.

In the next season we were paired with the big guns in the first round. But this time the outcome was much more acceptable to our fans. Our experience against Juventus probably stood us in good stead when we played the mighty Ajax, of Holland, and knocked them out 4-3 on aggregate in the European Cup.

I was disappointed to miss the first leg because of suspension but the return in Amsterdam was one of my most fulfilling football experiences. Ajax, like us, were cavalier and always tried to exhibit flair. They were the kind of team we liked meeting. From my seat in the stand the first match at Parkhead, drawn 2-2, was great excitement and Johan Cruyff was simply fabulous. He seemed to be everywhere. Today Cruyff is the Ajax coach and in May 1987 he guided them to a 1-0 victory over the East German club Lokomotiv Leipzig in the European Cup Winners Cup final in Athens. All the goals at Parkhead were scored in the first-half and this was our team:

Bonner, McGrain, Reid, Moyes, McAdam, MacLeod, Provan, McStay, McGarvey, Burns (Sullivan), Nicholas.

Celtic were down 1-0 to a goal by Olsen in only four minutes but the platform for a fight came when Tommy Burns was tripped by Cruyff. Swedish referee Erik Fredrikson gave a penatly and Charlie Nicholas scored. However, three minutes later Cruyff made amends for his penalty blunder by poking the ball to the Dane Lerby — the Ajax skipper — and he put them 2-1 in front with a chip over Bonner. Celtic levelled for a second time in 27 minutes. A Davie Moyes header beat the defence and Frank McGarvey hit the ball past the 'keeper as he came off his line. There might have been a second penalty when Burns was downed again — this time by Olsen. But the referee rejected appeals.

So to Amsterdam and I felt great being back in this side: Bonner, McGrain, Reid, Aitken, McAdam, Sinclair, Provan (McCluskey), McStay (Moyes), McGarvey, MacLeod, Nicholas. The pundits gave us little chance and even after the draw they pointed out that we would need a victory in Holland. Celtic promised to attack and we did despite all the usual European logic about caution away from home. A last-minute goal by sub George McCluskey gave us victory against all the odds. Long after the game was over at the Olympic Stadium hundreds of our fans stood on the terracings singing and dancing. Eventually we went out to acknowledge their enthusiasm. It was an emotional occasion. Billy McNeill ran on to the pitch at the end to hug each of us, he was so pleased with the win over a club of Ajax's calibre.

The honours went to Charlie Nicholas and McCluskey for scoring the goals — plus Bonner who was once again in smashing form. Charlie's goal in 33 minutes was a moment of magic. Graeme Sinclair had been detailed to shadow Cruyff but he was still able to make a crossfield pass from the left to Nicholas who stepped away from two tackles, pushed the ball to McGarvey, then chipped the return over the 'keeper. It was Cheeky Charlie at his very best.

Pressure in the second half was intense. Bonner had fine saves before being beaten by a freak. Vanenburg sent the ball across goal and it curled wickedly inside the post and rolled tantalisingly into the net. At that moment it seemed we were dead. But in 72 minutes Davie Provan was injured in a heavy tackle and had to be replaced by McCluskey who could have no inkling as he ran on that he was about to become Celtic's big hero. His goal came so late there was no time for Ajax to do anything about it. Celtic won on a 4-3 aggregate.

The second round took us to the Basque country of Spain and the picturesque seaside town of San Sebastian to meet Real Sociedad. This was our team: Bonner, McGrain, Aitken, McAdam, Reid, Sinclair, Provan, McStay, MacLeod, Nicholas, McGarvey. The Atocha Stadium was garish and noisy but I thought Celtic were composed and professional — until we found ourselves 2-0 down. Our hopes were shattered by two goals in four minutes of the second half by Satrustegui and Uralde. To add to our annoyance both were deflections. Sociedad, who had looked frustrated, were cock-a-hoop.

Sociedad had a burly defence — all by requirement Basques, by the way — and they had conceded only three goals in their previous seven Spanish League games. So we knew it was going to be tough in the second leg. The crowd at Parkhead was 54,874 and the scene was right for a Celtic fight-back. The players obliged but, unhappily, it was only 2-1, so Sociedad qualified on a 3-2 aggregate. It didn't console us any that the Spanish goal was really a gift from us. Celtic had ample chance to dispossess Sociedad on the lead-up to the goal which came in 25 minutes from Uralde. The ball was crossed into the six-yard box by World Cup star Ufarte, who should never have been given the opportunity to cross in the first place.

All of us played out of our skins that night. But Murdo MacLeod was our star man with two smash-hit goals. The first came from a Davie Provan free-kick which was touched into Murdo's path. He drove the ball home from all of 25 yards. Two minutes from the end Paul McStay manufactured a chance for MacLeod which he again took with style — and with his left foot. Our desperately disappointed team was: Bonner, McGrain, Reid (Burns), Aitken, McAdam, MacLeod, Provan (McCluskey), McStay, McGarvey, Sinclair, Nicholas.

Chapter 15

THIS MAN CLOUGH

BRIAN CLOUGH is an intriguing man. There are no half measures in his attitude to football, politics and life. He believes adamantly in quality on the pitch, votes Labour, threatened to stand for Parliament, is against blood sports and doesn't skimp on the luxuries of living.

You may not like the bold Brian, because he can be abrasive, but he cannot possibly be ignored and for many this runs to admiration. Any manager who can win the championship at Derby County and then move to Nottingham Forest to repeat the performance, with two European Cup final victories added, has unique credentials.

We expected the unexpected from Clough when Celtic tangled with Forest in the third round of the UEFA Cup. We were not disappointed. The day before we played at the City Ground he sent a message to Davie Hay inviting him to inspect the pitch because of changed conditions. Now, I ask you, how many opposing managers would offer such a courtesy? Davie Hay certainly couldn't resist the come-on. He went to the City Ground with chief scout John Kelman and backroom man Neil Mochan.

Neil played alongside Clough years ago in the Middlesbrough team when the Forest manager was knocking in goals before having to retire prematurely because of injury. Clough had made it clear he would like to see Neil again but he made one of his rare mistakes by at first thinking John was Neil. However, he quickly got it right and, anyway, it was understandable because neither uses Grecian 2000!

Clough not only showed the manager the pitch, he proceeded to hold court in one of his offices. He demanded to know if Davie Hay had a contract. He was told that Celtic managers never had contracts and this included the great Jock Stein. "Don't ever trust directors," said Clough impishly because two of our board — Jack McGinn, now the chairman, and Chris White — were present. "Get yourself a four-year deal."

Our directors realised Clough was stirring it so they didn't react. The manager just laughed and let Clough go on being provocative. He does it very well, too. "If I had been given the Rangers job when it was vacant — and I might well have been interested if anyone had asked — the first thing I would have done was sign four Celtic players," the bold Brian told an attentive and impromptu audience. "That would have sorted out the religious business at Ibrox once and for all."

To which Davie replied dryly: "I would have given you four Protestants!"

Nobody laughed louder than Clough because he was having everyone on.

When Forest came to Scotland for the second leg in December 1983, the team stayed at the Marine Hotel at Troon which is much favoured by the English when they play at Hampden. The Forest party were about 90 minutes late arriving and the Press were decidedly twitchy. What on earth could have happened to them?

I'll now let you into a secret. Driving from the airport the Forest coach passed a pub, then owned by Davie Hay, and this was indicated in bold letters above the door. Clough saw this as he passed on the coach and immediately called a halt. He ordered his players out and marched them into the pub, telling a shocked barman that the first round was on the Celtic manager. And it was. Brian simply doesn't take "no" for an answer.

That's the kind of unorthodox thing Clough does. I can think of no other club boss who would take the players drinking — mildly, of course — and get the opposing manager to pay.

The other side of Clough is his sheer professionalism and command of his job. We were to find out about this where it counts most — on the pitch. Some think there is nothing to football

Roy sprints in the Parkhead stand for the cameras.

management. They argue that it is all predictable. Clough knocks this theory on the head. His team and man management ideas are unique. They also work. He also says he likes Scots and former Scotland skipper Archie Gemmill is one of his favourites. Nevertheless, I often wonder what would have happened if Brian Clough *had* been given the job of Rangers manager.

We had to struggle through four games, however, before going to Nottingham and, by the way, that night even Rangers manager Jock Wallace came along to cheer us.

Our first stop was Aarhus in Denmark. It looked a difficult tie, with Danish football on an upswing. I scored the goal which gave us a 1-0 victory at home. Aarhus actually missed a penalty half an hour before I scored in the 63rd minute. As it turned out Aarhus weren't a great side but their defence was good and I was pleased to see my header going through the 'keeper's arms.

In Denmark Aarhus again defended in depth, often with ten players back. But we still won 4-1 with goals by Murdo MacLeod, Frank McGarvey, yours truly and Davie Provan. We really hammered them in the first half. Incidentally, that was the first time Celtic wore all-green outfits, which may well be a good omen as we qualified on a 5-1 aggregate.

In the second round we were paired with Sporting Lisbon and after losing 2-0 away from home we weren't given much chance. The forecasters of doom were again working overtime. Sporting had several splendid internationals, like the black flash Jordao and another veteran, Olivera. They gave us a drubbing in front of 70,000 at the Alvalade Stadium. Green-and-white flags fluttered from the crowd but these were also the colours of Sporting. Jordao scored in each half, the first in 30 minutes with help from his sparring mate Olivera.

The lightning Jordao, then 31, had twice suffered broken legs in his career but he gave no sign of this when he played us. His second goal came in 65 minutes, when he ran on to a pass from the half-way line and beat Tom McAdam for speed to tuck the ball into the back of the net. We certainly lived dangerously and yet another shot from Jordao actually bounced off Pat Bonner's legs — he was wearing a red jersey that night, by the way — and McAdam chased to the line to stop the ball. Our team that night: Bonner, McGrain, Sinclair, Aitken, McAdam, MacLeod, Provan, McStay, McGarvey, Burns, Melrose (McClair).

As usual we were told it would need a miracle for us to clinch the tie in the second leg. I thought to myself that there hadn't been too many of them in the last few centuries.

It turned out to be the best match I've played in at Parkhead. We won 5-0 with goals by Tommy Burns, Tom McAdam, Brian McClair, Murdo MacLeod and Frank McGarvey. A nice spread. It's games like this I like to remember most of all. Non-stop, flowing football — Celtic at their very best. Sporting were so surprised they didn't know what was going on.

Sporting were a really good team, as they had demonstrated in Lisbon. They collapsed, however, under our pressure. Everyone sizzled, including our fans who were even better and noisier than usual. At half-time we were 3-0 up but in the dressing-room we talked about the danger of losing a goal. However Murdo scored 12 minutes after half-time and that settled us. Our team: Bonner, McGrain, Sinclair, Aitken, McAdam, MacLeod, Provan, McStay, McGarvey (Melrose), Burns (Reid), McClair. One writer reported ecstatically: "Celtic turned an impossible dream into magnificent reality to write a fabulous glory chapter. Even the Lisbon Lions would have been proud of this amazing display." Praise indeed.

Interestingly, Celtic had only once before in their European history turned a two-goal deficit into victory. It was a super team effort but star billing went to McGarvey, McClair and Burns. We won 5-2 over the two games.

I will always remember this as a display of courage, determination and panache never bettered by Celtic in my time. Most who saw the game will agree and those who didn't can just accept this as the biased view of a contestant. Portugal are again in the forefront of European football and at that time they were also reasonably ranked. Certainly a club such as Sporting Lisbon were highly regarded throughout Europe.

And so to Nottingham on 23 November 1983. The only shaky Celtic spell was at the start and it took brave and brilliant work by Pat Bonner to avert a goal. He rescued Celtic in the 11th minute when McAdam missed a long ball out of Forest's defence. Birtles pounced to race in on us with only big Pat to beat. However, he ran out to smother the shot.

The ball was cleared upfield but suddenly the game had to be stopped as Celtic fans flooded on to the pitch. Play didn't resume for ten minutes as the Spanish referee tried to get order. However, it was quickly clear to us that this was no ordinary pitch invasion. The fans had been forced on to the field. At the particular area where Celtic fans were standing they seemed to be packed in like sardines. But, it was believed later, police opened a gate to allow more supporters in and it simply proved too much. Some were hurt but thankfully none seriously. It was a bad ten minutes.

Later Celtic were fined £2,000 for their part in this involuntary "invasion" of the pitch. However, on appeal Celtic established innocence and the £2,000 was refunded, minus £160 which was the penalty for a shoe and a toilet roll landing on the park.

Once the play restarted I didn't think we were ever in real danger. Forest 'keeper Steve Sutton was busier than Bonner. I reckoned it was to the credit of both teams that they overcame conditions. A third of the pitch was covered with white frost. Torvill and Dean, who come from Nottingham, would have liked the surface better than us. Paul McStay was a great midfield general for us that night and a lot of English managers who were guests at the match were talking about him afterwards. This included Billy McNeill.

Celtic's best attempt in the first half was a shot by the tireless Tommy Burns. I tried a long-ranger which Sutton failed to hold but in the scramble for the rebound McGarvey knocked the ball wide. Surprisingly, the referee played just over two minutes short in the first half. What a pity he didn't add it on in the second when we were in command and, I am sure, might have scored with just a little bit of extra time.

Celtic overcame all the problems, even an injury to Tom McAdam at the start of the second half. The absence of his skill and experience could have been a blow but when Jim Melrose came on Graeme Sinclair dropped back to the heart of the defence with me. This should have been Forest's chance to snatch the lead which Clough had said they needed. It never materialised.

Instead, Burns began a gem of a move and the ball was shuttled to McStay, then on to Brian McClair and Danny McGrain on the right. It was unfortunate that Jim Melrose blazed the final attempt over the bar. However, these things happen. Forest's frustration was demonstrated by the fact that Clough took off Peter Davenport and introduced one-time Scotland star Ian Wallace who, I seem to recall, wasn't getting on with the Forest manager at the time.

Celtic had settled quickly to the team switches and in truth could have gone back to Glasgow winning. These were the teams. *Forest:*

Sutton, Anderson, Swain, Fairclough, Hart, Bowyer, Wigley, Davenport (Wallace), Birtles, Hodge, Walsh. *Celtic:* Bonner, McGrain, Reid, Aitken, McAdam (Melrose), Sinclair, McClair, McStay, McGarvey, MacLeod, Burns. After a 0-0 draw our fans thought we were one game away from the quarter-finals. Clough warned differently but none of us was in any mood to listen to his brand of logic.

The crowd for the return — 66,938 — was fantastic. Brian Clough made no bones about saying he would love it if he could have such attendances at his City Ground. However, the game turned out to be too little too late for us. Forest were superbly disciplined at the back and their counter-attacking was equally good.

Most of Forest's good results had been away from home in that season so we knew it would be an even harder game at Parkhead. The 2-1 victory was their third away success in a row in the UEFA Cup. They played a 4-4-2 system similar to that of Aberdeen with wingers working back into the midfield. They had the clever Wigley and the very good Scot Colin Walsh who played the role well with Davenport and Birtles up front.

We never rose to the heights we should have done. Our disappointing form, indeed, made it easier for Forest. Our performance didn't begin to compare with the rout of Sporting Lisbon. Often I'm asked why this should happen. It is inexplicable and is down to players' attitudes and reactions on the night. Managers can do nothing about it, or very little, once the action begins.

Steve Hodge, whom Billy McNeill transferred from Aston Villa to Tottenham, and Walsh scored for Forest. We had a lot of hard luck but truthfully Forest deserved the victory. Clough had warned us before we left Nottingham — how nice of him! — that his No.7 would win the match in Glasgow. Well, I have to admit that Wigley ran 50 yards unmolested before crossing to Hodge who placed the ball in scorer Davenport's path. Then Davenport set up a second goal in 74 minutes, cutting the ball back to Walsh who swept it into the net. By the time Murdo MacLeod headed our consolation goal off McStay's corner the game was lost and we had only the agonising 1-2 aggregate scoreline to remember with considerable remorse. Here were the teams: *Celtic:* Bonner, McGrain, Reid, Aitken, McAdam, Sinclair (Melrose), McClair, McStay, McGarvey, MacLeod, Burns. *Forest:* Van Breukelen, Anderson, Swain, Fairclough, Hart, Bowyer,

Alan McInally, now with Aston Villa.

Wigley, Hodge, Birtles, Davenport, Walsh. By the way, in that season I played 51 competitive matches and also scored seven goals.

In season 1984-85 the Cup Winners Cup began quietly for Celtic with a 3-1 aggregate win over KAA Ghent. The Belgians beat us with a late goal by Cordiez in the first leg but at Parkhead it was straightforward with Frank McGarvey getting two goals and Paul McStay heading the other in the last minute. Teams — *Away:* Bonner, McGrain, Reid, Aitken, McAdam, MacLeod, Grant, McStay, McClair, Burns, McGarvey. *Home:* Bonner, McGrain,

MacLeod, Aitken, McAdam, Grant, Colquhoun (Provan), McStay, McClair, Burns, McGarvey.

The second round against Vienna Rapid was an entirely different matter and before the tie was settled we were to be involved in untold mayhem which, unhappily, was carried forward to the next season. In Vienna's Hanappi Stadium we lost 3-1 but that away goal meant that a 2-0 victory at Parkhead in the return would be good enough.

Tom McAdam was injured in training in Vienna. The Press didn't get the news until early morning so there was a lot of scurrying about before breakfast as they phoned the news that Willie McStay would be playing. As it turned out he did a good job in the back four. Behind us Pat Bonner was also in fine form. Willie McStay and Murdo MacLeod both had their names taken. Murdo's "offence" was the oddest of all. He moved away from our line-up as an Austrian was about to take a free-kick just outside the penalty box and was booked.

When the kick was in fact taken Murdo ran out of defence and pushed the ball forward at which point Alan McInally, who had come on as a substitute for his first European game and who had no other foul against him, was red-carded for hurling himself at Hans Pregesbauer. The Austrian lay on the ground as if requiring the Last Rites but got up quickly when he saw that McInally was being sent to the dressing-room.

Danny McGrain also received a second caution in the competition which meant he couldn't play in the second leg. We realised as the Bulgarian referee held up the yellow card that the absence of Danny, with all his experience, would seriously disadvantage us.

The referee had oddly ignored the fact that Reinhard Kienast booted Frank McGarvey in the early minutes and put him out of the match. He also later ignored a flying tackle by the same player on McInally who had replaced Frank. I mentioned earlier about the unexplained hate relationship between Scotland and Austrian teams and these tackles were merely further confirmation.

The Austrians were a good, but not a great side. The veteran defender Antonin Panenka was important to them but at 36 he had to pace himself carefully. Brian McClair had earlier levelled the score at 1-1 with some help from Paul McStay and Alan McInally, and even at 2-1 Celtic's job looked routine for the match at Parkhead, though an 87th-minute goal by the international veteran Hans Krankl put a new complexion on our task. *Celtic*: Bonner, W.

McStay, MacLeod, Aitken, McAdam, Grant, Provan, P. McStay, McClair, Burns (Reid), McGarvey.

The return game in Glasgow has already entered into European folklore. Celtic won 3-0 which meant an aggregate victory of 4-3. We had every reason to feel pleased except for the fact that it was one of the unruliest games ever seen in Scotland. Celtic were viciously punished because of an incident over which the club had no control.

The Austrians were so jittery and bad-tempered it was incredible and the Swedish referee, Kjell Johansson, was barely able to keep control. The worst trouble came ten minutes from the end when we were leading 3-0. There was what I considered a clear penalty incident for a foul by the reserve 'keeper, Karl Ehn, on Tommy Burns. Remarkably the referee wasn't sure and went over to the linesman who was flagging furiously in front of the "Jungle".

An experienced European referee should have understood the dangers of this and called the linesman towards him. Instead he went right to the touchline and stood there chatting, with Austrians milling around them. It was a clearly provocative situation although I am not in any way defending what happened. Merely trying to explain it.

While the match officials were talking — and it seemed to be for an eternity — substitute Rudolph Weinhofer fell down and in the row which followed other players claimed he had been struck by a bottle. There is no doubt one was thrown from the terracing. It made me sick that this should have happened.

I could see right away the Austrians were trying to maximise the incident, sensing a way first to avoid the penalty and then, more importantly, to have the game replayed. The referee picked up the bottle, walked across the pitch and handed it to an official near the dugout. Skipper Krankl, meantime, motioned to the other players to go off. It was then that I sensed their cunning. They were out of the competition — unless they could rubbish the game altogether. Had the referee beckoned the linesman to him the incident would never have taken place. Certainly there would have been no bottle-throwing.

Weinhofer went off like a man wounded in a war, which brought the Austrians down to nine players. He was the second of their subs and Kienast had earlier been sent off for an off-the-ball foul on Burns which was spotted by a linesman. The fact that a player went off the pitch because of an injury was to be crucial when the case went before UEFA.

In action behind "closed doors".

TV pictures showed that, while a bottle was thrown, it most certainly did not strike any Austrian. Weinhofer left the ground later with a huge bandage round his head as if he had been hit by a sledge-hammer. An ambulanceman, Eddie McGarrell, who treated the Austrian, said there wasn't a mark of either bruises or bleeding and the player was fully conscious. It was gamesmanship at its most obvious. Nothing will ever convince me otherwise.

Eventually, after nearly 15 minutes, the referee awarded a penalty to Celtic but, not surprisingly after all the arguing and rowing, Peter Grant shot the ball wide.

The dreadful scene had been totally avoidable. First of all it was a mystery to me how the referee didn't see that Burns had been fouled. This would have meant a penalty being given without further ado. However, the doubt in his mind should have been clarified by calling the linesman half-way to meet him thus taking the scene of the indecision a distance away from the irate fans. It was provocative to be debating in this way, with Austrian players jostling angrily, so close to the crowd. There had been no hint of such trouble earlier. The referee took Zlatko Krankjcar's name for a foul on Murdo MacLeod and then everything seemed to settle. Our first goal came in 32 minutes. Paul McStay pushed the ball forward to Davie Provan for a cross to the far post which allowed Brian McClair to whip the ball into goal. MacLeod snatched the second in time added on by the referee for first-half stoppages. Provan had sent the ball in to the penalty area for Murdo to finish off with a volley.

The bitter row really began in the 68th minute when Burns grabbed No. 3. A shot by McGarvey was fumbled and dropped by the 'keeper. Burns rushed in to shoot home with the goalie kneeling on the ground. Ehn protested that he had been fouled and so did most of his team-mates. But the referee was firm and the goal stood. Krankl was booked for his protests and two minutes later Kienast was red-carded.

In fact, the second half ran for an hour. This was because of the time which had to be added on to allow for the hullabaloo kicked up by the Austrians. Celtic's industry won a match which unfortunately was to be remembered for all the wrong reasons. Our team that night: Bonner, W. McStay, MacLeod, Aitken, McAdam, Grant, Provan, P. McStay, McClair, Burns (Reid), McGarvey.

Ironically, on that same night former Celt Kenny Dalglish was sent off as Liverpool lost to Benfica in Portugal by a penalty goal but they went through to the next round of the European Cup on a 3-2 aggregate.

However, things went from bad to worse for us. Rapid arrogantly demanded that we should be thrown out of Europe. They wanted the result at Parkhead overturned and the tie awarded to them. When UEFA's Disciplinary Committee met Celtic were fined £4,000 and Rapid £6,000. In addition Rapid's coach Otto Baric was banned from three European games because of his violent protests. In fact, at one point he heaved the offending bottle back on to the pitch in a fit of rage. Ordered-off Kienast was suspended for four games. And, most important, Weinhofer's claim that he had been hit by a bottle was dismissed. This to me meant that Rapid had been found guilty of a blatant attempt to cheat their way into the next round. Our late chairman, Desmond White, said of the UEFA decision: "I honestly feel Celtic Football Club have been exonerated and I am satisfied that justice appears to have been done."

However, our relief was short-lived. Rapid appealed and UEFA about-turned in an extraordinary way and ordered a third game. Rapid had changed their story and claimed Weinhofer had been hit by a "small, unidentified object". They said they thought it was a coin. UEFA's ruling that the game had to be replayed was unbelievable. Baric, seeing his opportunity, had made sure Weinhofer came off the pitch at Parkhead. Since a player had already been sent off this meant they had to play the last ten minutes with nine players as Weinhofer was the second substitute. Rapid had their fine upped to £10,000, which made the decision to order a third match all the more confusing.

The third game at Old Trafford was a fiasco. We lost 1-0 and it was no consolation that Rapid were jeered off the park. Our 3-0 victory at Parkhead was wiped out and so the most unsporting, unruly lot it has been my misfortune to oppose were winners over two games by 4-1.

A misguided few of our supporters, completely incensed by what had gone before, let us down by attacking the Austrian 'keeper Herbert Feurer and Peter Pacult as the players fled for the dressing-room at the end. It was to cost Celtic dearly the next season. The sad thing for the club, the players and the fans was that a few hotheads caused so much havoc and got away with it. Nobody in his or her right mind would do anything like this if they realised the harm it would cause to a club they allegedly support.

We performed disappointingly at Old Trafford. It was all too much of an anti-climax. If UEFA had made the third game a one-off, winner-take-all job, then I feel sure we would have done better. Pacult scored a 17th-minute goal just after I had hit a post at the other end. It wasn't our night. Or, for that matter, our season in Europe. The Celtic players on that dreadful night were: Bonner, McGrain, MacLeod, Aitken, McAdam (Colquhoun), Grant, Provan, McStay, McGarvey, Burns, McClair. None of them will thank me for reminding them that they took part.

UEFA's reaction to the attacks on two players at Old Trafford was to fine the club £17,000 and order the next European game at Parkhead to be played behind closed doors. Hard though the punishment seemed, it could have been worse. UEFA said they took into account the previous good behaviour of Celtic fans who had watched European football in all but one season over a 23-year period. SFA secretary Ernie Walker had also written to UEFA before the Manchester match pointing out the hostility which had been built up by a third game — and the tension this had created.

Celtic's Board were given 48 hours to appeal but were unanimous that this would be counter-productive. It was better to accept it, believing that sportsmanship extended to legislative areas as well as just the pitch. A club statement said: "The club did everything possible to guard against trouble at the third match in Manchester. Now there is a price to be paid. Both ourselves and UEFA now want to put the Rapid affair behind us."

Eight months later — on 18 September 1985 — Celtic resumed European competition in the Cup Winners Cup in Madrid. The opposition, Atletico Madrid, were formidable.

Celtic fought back for a 1-1 draw and Mo Johnston notched his first goal in Europe for the club. Pat Bonner was another hero. He saved a 76th-minute penalty which was his fourth exceptional stop of the match at the Calderon Stadium in front of 55,000. The Spaniard, Enrique Setien, had his name taken for a bad tackle on Peter Grant. Davie Provan and Paul McGugan were also yellow-carded — Provan for gesturing angrily at the referee. However, there was no serious trouble and this pleased us almost as much as our performance.

We saw the two faces of Atletico. They attacked in the first half, scored through Setien, and then sat in afterwards to defend this slim lead. Back-pedalling they looked vulnerable. Certainly, we couldn't

Pat Bonner looks happy with Brian McClair just getting into the picture.

believe our good luck. Their tactics seemed to be wrong but there was no way we were going to point this out to them! Earlier they had been socking it to us, bringing out the best in Bonner. He saved with his legs from Da Silva, stopped another after the same player had beaten Danny McGrain, and then two-handed the ball over the bar from Atreche. The Spaniards shook their heads in disbelief and clearly wondered how they were going to beat big Pat. However, Setien did so in 35 minutes with a 15-yard angled shot as he came in from the left.

Celtic's equaliser was the end product of tenacious play by Peter Grant. The surprised Spaniards backed away like boxers trying to avoid a KO. When the ball was pushed out to Provan he ran for the line and crossed superbly. Johnston's head flashed at the far post and the ball flew away from Argentina's World Cup goalie, Fillol.

The penalty save was almost as exciting as the equaliser. McGugan, who had stopped a certain goal in the first half, tackled substitute Rubio just inside the area. The Spaniard hurled himself to the ground. The West German referee, Volker Roth, pointed to the spot. In the ensuing hubbub Rubio himself placed the ball, gave himself a ten-step run-up, and hit the ball viciously close to Bonner's right-hand post. Big Pat lunged instinctively and made one of the best saves of his career. One of our leading sportswriters summed up the performance as "a credit to Celtic and Scotland".

The return at Parkhead highlighted the importance of our fans — in their absence. It was like playing in a graveyard with no supporters present. The ghostly silence was deafening. However, this was us paying the penalty for the action of a few louts. We lost that day 2-1 and 3-2 over the tie, and Celtic still hadn't managed to knock a Spanish side out of Europe. The cash loss to Celtic was in excess of £250,000 and, more important, it was an inglorious exit.

Frankly, we were disappointing. Minus our partisan support it was one of our poorest shows for some time. We deserved to lose and even manager Davie Hay admitted to the Press: "The lack of atmosphere worked against us but Atletico were first to the ball and we simply never got going. The game showed what the fans mean to Celtic. They were sorely missed. We couldn't string passes together and, if a team doesn't succeed in this department, it's obvious what's going to happen."

Louis Aragones, the Atletico coach, twice had to be told by the police to return to his dugout. He claimed arrogantly at the end that his team had controlled the game "from beginning to end". I thought this was an exaggeration. Celtic had a purple patch midway through the first half and just a few minutes before the Spaniards struck their first KO blow with a goal by Setien, Peter Grant had chased and caught the ball at the by-line and whipped it briskly across goal where Murdo MacLeod did everything right until he hit the ball and it spun over the bar.

Friends told me later that Spanish commentators in the Press box, which is high above our stand, made more noise than the rest of the spectators — officials and reporters only — as they machine-gunned their words to Madrid. In fact, microphones seemed superfluous when Setien curled the ball away from Bonner.

Some people thought Celtic looked like a side in a dress rehearsal and saving their best for the real thing. But this was it.

Nearly 20 minutes into the second half Celtic tried to change the balance of the game by moving me into midfield. Atletico's answer was a Da Silva "goal" which was disallowed by the Italian referee for offside. But in 71 minutes there was a genuine strike by Quique who went past McAdam and McGrain before beating Bonner. A couple of minutes later, after good work by Danny and Brian McClair, I was able to flick in the cut-back. But we needed two more goals and, with such a limited time available, this was clearly beyond us.

As we trooped off in despair feeling that all things being even we were better than Rapid Vienna or Atletico Madrid despite the outcome, I hoped we would never again have to play with none of our fans watching. Professional football is about people and entertainment. We felt hopelessly inadequate without our "twelfth man". Our teams — *Away:* Bonner, McGrain, Burns, Aitken, McGugan, Grant, Provan, McStay, Johnston, MacLeod, McClair. *Home:* Bonner, McGrain (McInally), Burns, Aitken, McGugan, Grant, Provan, McStay (McAdam), Johnston, MacLeod, McClair.

As Premier League champions we moved into the European Cup again in season 1985-86. Our first jaunt was to Dublin to meet Shamrock Rovers and we were fully aware it would be a difficult match. In fact, Rovers were inspired. It was the Republic of Ireland's biggest football occasion of the season and the Shamrock boyos certainly rose to it. A spectacular goal by Murdo MacLeod eight minutes from the end gave us a win but the truth was Pat Bonner had to be at his very best in his home country.

Murdo's goal stunned the Irish crowd. They were in festive mood and extra seats had been put into the ground to accommodate the all-ticket crowd. Shamrock goalie Jodi Byrne had no chance at all with Murdo's shot from 16 yards on the run. The ball swirled away from the goalkeeper and we all had the feeling that the glory which Shamrock fought so hard to achieve on their own territory went with it. Shamrock, for their part, were annoyed with themselves because Mick Byrne, their striker, could easily have scored a couple of times in the first few minutes of the second half.

There were some bizarre happenings but happily no serious trouble. Union Jacks were burned in the crowd before the kick-off and later UEFA fined Shamrock for this. Fans also climbed floodlit pylons and raced along the enclosure roof.

Twice Celtic hit the woodwork, Brian McClair in the first half and Mo Johnston in the second with a 25-yard shot against the right-hand post. Shamrock brimmed over with energy as you would expect. But Danny McGrain, who had been brought into the side, didn't flinch. Paul McGugan was injured in only five minutes but he stayed on the pitch for a further 25 minutes before being replaced by Pierce O'Leary who, of course, once played for Shamrock. *Celtic:* Bonner, W. McStay, McGrain, Aitken, McGugan (O'Leary), Grant, McClair, P. McStay, Johnston, MacLeod, Burns. *Shamrock Rovers:* J. Byrne, Neville, Brady, Keely, Eccles, P. Byrne, Cody, Larkin, M. Byrne, Doolin, O'Brien.

Immediately before the second game there were newspaper reports that Manchester United were interested in Mo Johnston. He denied adamantly any knowledge of this. Anyway, the fans demonstrated that night that they very much wanted him to stay and he replied with goals in the 27th and 61st minutes. With 20 minutes to go Johnston was subbed and he was away from the ground before the final whistle, which let him avoid questions from reporters. However, he did say he didn't want to leave the club.

Owen Archdeacon took Johnston's place but by that time the game was well and truly won. Johnston's first goal was clinical finishing of a move begun by Murdo MacLeod and continued by Brian McClair and Alan McInally. In front of goal Johnston demonstrated the accuracy others had been lacking despite the fact that Shamrock packed their defence on the instructions of player-manager Dermot Keely, who played with a heavily bandaged knee. It was Mo's sheer striker's instinct which put him in the right place to finish off. Willie McStay's cross was just perfect for him to score

Mo Johnston has just missed a chance. Brian Whittaker, of Hearts is beside him.

his second with a header. The ball sailed gracefully into goal and the Celtic fans were so delighted they were in a state of near apoplexy.

Our midfield of Murdo MacLeod, Paul McStay and Tony Shepherd were too good for the Irish and Johnston had too much pace and skill for the big defenders Peter Eccles and Kevin Brady. Celtic went through on a 3-0 aggregate. *Celtic:* Bonner, W. McStay, Burns, Aitken, Whyte, MacLeod, McClair (McGhee), McStay, Johnston (Archdeacon), Shepherd, McInally. *Shamrock Rovers:* J. Byrne, Neville, Brady, Keely, Eccles, P. Byrne. Coady, Larkin, M. Byrne, Doolin, O'Brien.

Two days later we were told our second-round opponents and meeting Dinamo Kiev was like opposing two-thirds of Russia's World Cup eleven. It was certainly an exciting prospect. Dinamo were immediately made favourites because of their outstanding record in the Soviet Union as well as of the individual members of their team in Mexico.

Dinamo sent a two-man deputation ahead to study our play so they went into the game on 22 October 1986 knowledgeable about our players and style. However, in front of an enthusiastic crowd of 47,858 we managed only a 1-1 draw and that away goal by the Russians was clearly a major danger to us for the return. In the event of a tie it would count as two. We were given a lot of plaudits for our performance but we were immediately aware that a goalless draw in the second match would be good enough to send Dinamo to the next round.

They were ritzy Reds, all right. Six of the players were World Cup participants. They showed exceptional tactical expertise. In fact, they were probably the best team to visit Scotland in the whole season, with no disrespect intended either to Dundee United, who played Barcelona and Borussia Munchengladbach, or to Rangers who also met the same West German club.

Dinamo grabbed a goal through Vadim Yevtushenko in 17 minutes It was a disaster for Pat Bonner and a rare one at that. The ball broke to Yevtushenko from a corner. Bonner had a careful eye on him as he moved in. But the ball took an awkward bounce, squirmed away from Pat and the Soviet turned it in at the far post.

We certainly needed luck against Dinamo and we got only one slice of it, with 11 minutes of the game to go. Murdo MacLeod lofted the ball into the penalty area. Mo Johnston was there, ready and waiting. He struck it against the tall goalie Viktor Chanov and, obligingly, the ball spun back to Mo. The second time he made no mistake. The ball whizzed past Chanov.

Celts made other chances but it would be unsporting not to concede we were against class opposition — although not the best we have met. We were upset a bit by a 20th-minute injury to Tommy Burns. He was badly fouled by Alexander Zavarov. He limped off and was replaced by Mark McGhee. Tommy couldn't even play in the second leg two weeks later. He travelled with us on the charter plane but there was never any chance of him playing. The side which got the draw was: Bonner, Grant, Burns (McGhee), Aitken, Whyte, MacLeod, McClair, McStay, Johnston, Shepherd, McInally. We took a lot of heart out of the game and genuinely thought we had a chance in the return.

We were quite excited about going to Kiev which is only about 50 kilometres from Chernobyl where the worst nuclear disaster ever to hit the world unhappily took place. Beforehand there was a lot of discussion about whether or not Celtic should go. But all the reports and advice from the Foreign Office were that we should travel. And when we did it was by Aeroflot, the Russian national airline.

I was certain there would be no danger to us from radiation. Clearly, the Russians wouldn't want to risk this because of the further world-wide adverse publicity it would have entailed. There was no evidence at all in Kiev itself that anything had gone so badly wrong just months before. People went about their business apparently normally. However, I was told that hundreds of families were still temporarily housed in Kiev, which is a handsome city of old and new, capital of the Ukraine and, the locals said, is more hospitable than Moscow.

The BBC's Soviet correspondent, Brian Hanrahan, came from Moscow. He explained that he had been trying for some months to get permission to visit the Ukraine. The Celtic game had made this possible for him. Soviet citizens, and more particularly foreign nationals in Russia, don't have the freedom of movement which exists in Britain. However, the people of Kiev with whom we came in contact were friendly and helpful.

Tim Kelly, a hotel manager well known to both Celtic and Rangers, travelled with us. He brought special food supplies with him — cheese, tinned meats and fish, and chocolate. So there was never any chance of us going hungry.

As I mentioned, Kiev is an attractive city with universities, museums and opera houses. As we entered we saw the 120-metres-high stainless steel statue of the Mother of Kiev welcoming visitors. To be honest, she didn't have a particularly friendly face but the Soviets themselves joked about this. It is a superb piece of craftsmanship. While there we also saw the Soviet forces parading to celebrate the revolution. It was an impressive sight.

I really thought we threatened doom for Dinamo for at least some of the game at the huge Republic Stadium in front of a crowd of 100,000. Many more wanted to see the game but there was simply no more room. Russian players incidentally, are still technically amateurs but Dinamo had all sorts of privileges not available to the workers. Their fans certainly went mutinously silent when Celtic did anything particularly clever. Late in the match Dinamo were even down to time wasting, which indicates how anxious they were as we made our last stand.

My personal disappointment was that a 3-1 defeat clinched Dinamo's quarter-final place. It was the sixth time we had failed to get to the last eight. As I've said already, I want to help put this right.

Youngsters like Tony Shepherd, Peter Grant and Derek Whyte took a lot out of this match. Derek had a particularly tough time but, remembering he was only 18, it was a good performance and he can only benefit in the future. In the second half Danny McGrain didn't come out and he was replaced by Pierce O'Leary.

Celtic had to overcome the setback of a 12th-minute goal by Oleg Blokhin. We did so with some style and Dinamo, at least temporarily, lost some of their passing accuracy and flair. As I tried to stir things up from the midfield Murdo MacLeod slogged it out gallantly in defence. The scoring began when Whyte conceded a foul just outside the penalty box. Andrei Bal tried to take it too quickly and he was booked by the Austrian referee. In the retake Vladimir Bessonov went off on a decoy run and Blokhin followed up to curl the ball past Pat Bonner with his very good left foot.

In 31 minutes Paul McStay lashed in a left-foot shot which hit off a post and bounced into Chanov's arms. Celtic kept their heads at this critical time. Several times we came close to equalising and finally we did so four minutes after the interval. Murdo MacLeod made a run from defence, passed to Brian McClair, who made a superb square cross for Mark McGhee to sweep the ball into goal for his first Euro success since joining Celtic.

In the second half we used three at the back and pushed an extra

Derek Whyte, arms outstretched, races away from an attacker.

man forward. It was all or nothing and we knew it. However, though this seemed to be working, a misjudged header led to the ball breaking to the alert Pavel Yacovenko who sent it soaring high into goal. Celtic claimed he was offside but the referee wouldn't listen. Soon after Mark had his name taken for protesting.

When the Soviets grabbed a third goal it was set up by Blokhin. He beat Whyte and cut the ball across for Vadim Yevtushenko to finish off dramatically. We hurled ourselves into the final action and in the last two minutes Johnston and MacLeod could both have scored. Our team: Bonner, McGrain, MacLeod, Aitken, Whyte, Grant, McClair, McStay, Johnston, Shepherd, McGhee. As we flew home the *Daily Record* was already giving its view: "Despite the score Celtic emerged with considerable credit."

I was very surprised that Dinamo, the favourites to win the trophy, were later bundled out by the unfancied Portuguese team Porto. Trailing 2-1 from the first leg in the semi-final the Soviets lost by the same score in front of their own disbelieving fans and crashed 4-2 on aggregate.

Chapter 16

MY FINEST TEAMS

ONE day I hope to be a manager. To prepare me for this I have been attending the SFA's coaching classes and I feel this will stand me in good stead in the future. Certainly one of the greatest challenges I would face as a manager would be choosing the right blend of players. It might be of interest, then, if I now have a go at team-picking — the best Celtic side drawn from players of my era, the best Scotland international eleven and the best from the last World Cup in Mexico. Not everyone will agree with me, of course, but argument is one of the great facets of the game because we can all debate into infinity and usually all finish up right if it's a matter of opinion.

Modesty forces me to omit myself although there have been some very successful player-managers lately. My Celtic team will line up 4-4-2 and is: Bonner, McGrain, Stanton, McAdam, Lynch, McStay, Provan, Dalglish, Nicholas, Burns, Lennox.

The big shock, I suppose, is that I pass over Brian McClair and Mo Johnston. However, Kenny Dalglish and Charlie Nicholas are my men. I might have found a midfield role for Brian because I feel this is where he is best. I could have a front two of Dalglish and Nicholas with McClair behind them. However, this would mean leaving out either Tommy Burns or Paul McStay and changing the style to 4-3-3. My original plan strikes me as being more effective. So, sorry Brian, you're on the bench. And beside him I'd be picking from Murdo MacLeod, Derek Whyte, Frank McGarvey and Ronnie Glavin.

My two wide players, coming from the middle, would be Davie Provan and Bobby Lennox. They would move up and down the flanks but would also be required to come inside to cover.

My centre-half is also controversial but I never thought Tom McAdam got the credit he deserved. He played around 350 games for Celtic, mostly as a defender, although he signed in September 1977, from Dundee United, for £60,000 as a forward. Around that period Celtic also recruited John Dowie from Fulham, Francis Munro from Wolves and Joe Fillippi from Ayr United. Tom was easily the most successful buy. I enjoyed playing beside him. Roddie MacDonald was the other centre-half at that time but I didn't play as often with him. McAdam was criticised quite a lot but I thought he was good and didn't deserve most of it. He was exceptional in the air.

Pat Stanton was a great safety valve for us. He signed in September 1976, and it was no coincidence that we won our tenth League and Cup double in a season in which Jock Stein also returned to full fitness. The Championship was settled at Easter Road when we still had four games to play. Being a former Hibs skipper, Pat found this very satisfying although I know he always had a soft spot for the Edinburgh club. Pat played 36 League games and seven cup-ties in that very memorable season. When he signed I was pushed into the middle of the park. Big Roddie was behind me and my role was as defensive midfielder. I remember Pat as a player who made everything look so simple.

Choosing my goalie was easy. Pat Bonner has been a tremendous player for Celtic. A 'keeper will always make mistakes — it even happens to Pat at times — but I feel his consistency, especially in the last couple of seasons, has been excellent. Pat is a great talker on the pitch. He never leaves the men in front of him in any doubt when it's his ball. I also have a high regard for Peter Latchford who, ironically, first came to the park in February 1975, on the same day Jock Stein was named assistant to Scotland manager Willie Ormond. Peter has, of course, been freed and it was sad to see him go because he is a cheery bloke to have around as well as being a good goalie.

A player with everything ahead of him is Derek Whyte. At the moment he may not be ruthless enough at centre-half but this will

Paul McStay steers the ball past Dougie Bell and Steve Cowan of Hibs.

come. He certainly has the football talent. Still in defence, Andy Lynch was really reliable at left-back. This has been a hard position to fill at Parkhead since the departure of Tommy Gemmell. Mark Reid, for instance, is a smashing player and is doing well now with Charlton. But he knew he was that little bit short of pace. He may well have left Celtic too quickly but I certainly thought he had a good left foot, although not good enough to edge into my team!

Bobby Lennox played the left-wing position for Celtic for so long he became a fixture. He is my best pal in the game and was brilliant coming in from the wing to play off the front. He also won the bronze boot as Europe's third-highest scorer. My team is of course geared to score goals, in the parlance of managers, and what a couple of subs I have on the bench in McClair and Johnston.

The most remarkable Celt of all, of course, is Danny McGrain. In my time, that is. How sad that he has now left Parkhead after such a fine career. The place won't be the same without him. I am sure, however, that Danny will be a good investment for Hamilton Accies.

With me as manager — go on, laugh! — I feel this team would win the Premier League next season. However, we would have to do some turning back of the clock.

I hope myself to play on until well into my 30s. It is always difficult to forecast but this is my intention at the age of 28. Football is really all I know. So I would also like to stay in the game when I am over the hill as a player. Some don't relish the challenge of being a manager but I certainly do. I've also toyed with the idea, once my playing days are over, of having an interest in insurance or investment.

There will be more rows about my best Scots team and I emphasise I am confining my choice to players of my own time. Here is my élite eleven, in 4-4-2 again: Leighton, McGrain, Miller, McLeish, Malpas, Strachan, Souness, Dalglish, Robertson, Nicholas Jordan. My bench men would come from McQueen, Rough, Hansen, Davie Cooper, Sharp and Gough.

You may think John Robertson is a surprise. He shouldn't really be. Jock Stein adulated Robertson and so did Brian Clough when he was his player with Nottingham Forest. Robertson was a natural wide left midfielder. He came deep to pick the ball up and then would run to the by-line and make crosses. He was the classic crosser of a ball to the far post and made a lot of goals for his strikers in this

Two great rivals and friends — Derek Johnstone and Danny McGrain.

way. He is one of the most deceptive players I can recall. He always looked done in but when he got the ball he went past the full-back as if he wasn't there.

The question will be: Why not Davie Cooper? He probably has more ability than Robertson but I have always felt he lacks consistency although he is a great player.

My defensive anchor men are Jim Leighton, Willie Miller and Alex McLeish. Why not? Miller and McLeish kept me out of the Scots team for years. Jock Stein told me when I was playing centre-half or sweeper at Parkhead that he couldn't fit me into the Scotland team because he didn't want to split up such a good Aberdeen partnership. I understood this. When I got back it was in the midfield and that's where I've played most of my games in the dark blue jersey. To keep a club partnership on in the national team is good thinking. And the fact is that Leighton, Miller and McLeish have the best defensive record in Europe over the years.

Danny McGrain is obviously my right-back and Maurice Malpas goes in on the left. I've played with Frank Gray and Willie Donnachie but prefer the Dundee United man.

Graeme Souness's international career may now be over but I would still have him in my side. He is always available no matter what is going on. He wants the ball. Similarly, Kenny Dalglish and Gordon Strachan are obvious choices in the midfield and surely this illustrates the Liverpool boss's versatility as I have picked him as a striker for Celtic.

I have picked big Joe Jordan up front because I believe he frightened the opposition. And especially when he took his teeth out! Jaws had nothing on Joe. What a nice guy, but this is one striker I wouldn't like to have opposed. Wee Charlie would have revelled with Joe alongside him and Robertson supplied the kind of crosses Joe loved. He was far from a prolific scorer with Scotland but I reckon he took the strain off others and made openings for them with his abrasive style.

If Andy Roxburgh could field this team in the future I don't think he would have many problems. However, my view will never be put to the test.

Picking from the world provides such a broad canvas that it is confusing. There are so many really good players from whom to select. Here goes again: Shilton (England), Josimar (Brazil), Julio Cesar (Brazil), Bossi (France), Amoros (France), Platini (France),

Mo Johnston challenged by Graeme Souness.

Arnesen (Denmark), Magath (West Germany), Lineker (England), Laudrup (Denmark), Maradona (Argentina). I reckon this lot, if they could have been brought together, would have walloped any side in the world, including Maradona's champions. I mean Argentina, not Naples, whom the best player in the world today has led to the Italian championship.

I select Peter Shilton as my goalie because of his remarkable consistency over a long number of years. Rinat Dassayev, of the Soviet Union, would be next on my list but I wouldn't bother about Harald Schumacher, of West Germany, because of his ludicrous tackle on Patrick Battiston, of France, in the 1982 series in Spain.

Josimar was a newcomer to Brazil's team. So much so that he was a very late choice. But he was the kind of gem the Brazilians never fail to throw up in the World Cup. Felix-Wolfgang Magath impressed me as a playmaker for West Germany. He controlled the games for them.

Frank Arnesen and Maradona could complement each other with one supporting and the other filling in. Wee Maradona likes to get the ball deep and the things he does with it after that are just magic.

Diego is a rarity. Everyone, or very nearly, had a go at comparing him with Pele of Brazil but they are different types in separate eras. He is the poor little boy from the back streets of Buenos Aires who is estimated to have made £3 million in endorsements and other promotional perks after Mexico. However, Maradona has never forgotten his own poor beginnings and has done a lot of splendid work for UNICEF, the fund which helps poor kids around the globe.

Interestingly, Maradona picked out Michael Laudrup, who has been playing for Juventus in Italy, as one of the best players in Mexico. I am glad he has endorsed my opinion. I considered Laudrup and Arnesen to be outstanding when they played us in Mexico.

Chapter 17

THE GANG OF FOUR

WHEN Billy McNeill returned to Parkhead he knew changes would have to be made following a barren season. He did not, however, expect to have to replace Brian McClair, Mo Johnston, Alan McInally and Murdo MacLeod in one go. Mick McCarthy had already been purchased from Manchester City but this was to remedy a weakness in defence which had long been acknowledged. So our manager's job could not have been more difficult and especially as other clubs, aware of Celtic's predicament, set prices which were difficult to meet. Clubs in Scotland also now try to sell players in England or abroad rather than have them appearing in Celtic or Rangers jerseys against them at least four times in a season.

In his first period as Celtic manager Billy McNeill did a slick refurbishing job and, naturally, Celtic supporters are confident that, given reasonable time, he will do so again. We would like to think that Andy Walker will be as successful as the manager's last purchase from Motherwell, Brian McClair. But one lesson learned about the new freedom of contracts scheme, from the club's point of view, surely is that it is unwise to have three strikers — McClair, Johnston and McInally — all with contracts ending at the same time.

From the players' viewpoint freedom of contract works well,

although I feel time for decisions on both sides could be more precisely defined. But McClair and Johnston will be missed particularly. Scorers like them are not exactly plentiful. Manchester United have made a good buy because Brian was Celtic's top scorer for four years and this is why the manager insisted he didn't want to sell him.

It looked for a long time last season as though Brian would be the first Scot to win the European Golden Boot Award but he was overtaken on the run-in. He is a fine player but I will surprise you with the inside information that he is what I call "slack" in training. Yet he knocks his pan in every time he runs on to the park for a match. His work rate is tremendous and particularly when he is coming from behind the front two. This is the position I feel he likes best.

In training he is slow and usually is at the back of the pack. I've always believed a player has to put the same amount of energy into preparation as he will expend in matches but Brian belies this. His standard of natural fitness is simply exceptionally high. His speciality is running at opponents with the ball at his feet. He has good close control and pace and is also very strong. He is better coming from the middle. In this way he has to run on to balls more. He likes the play in front of him. A good example was the goal he scored in the Skol Cup final. I knocked the ball to Mo Johnston and he hit it back for Brian to run on to it. He struck the ball beautifully into the top left hand corner. He proved here what a great striker of the ball he can be. His backswing, in the parlance of Jack Nicklaus, is short but he clips the ball fiercely and accurately.

Despite all this Mo was always much more in the full publicity glare. It was because of the kind of guy Wee Mo is. He can't do anything quietly — as the fans of French club Nantes will find out! — whereas Brian does most things without swank. His private life is just that. I don't think Brian and Mo have anything in common apart from the ability to score goals. They are very different people.

It didn't surprise me last season when the Scottish Football Writers' Association made Brian their Player of the Year and the players also made him their No. 1 choice. Mind you, Brian was also the PFA chairman which must have helped!

Last season, in fact, Brian achieved so many milestones he began to look like one. Although he has left the club I feel it is fair to put them on record. In November 1986, he started a Celtic League game

Mo Johnston, the ball at his feet, with Brian McClair in support.

for the 100th time and scored in the 1-1 draw with Rangers. In December, a goal at Fir Park was his 100th in all competitions for the club and also established him as Celtic's best Premier League scorer, passing Frank McGarvey's tally of 77. McClair scored four goals in the Premier League on three occasions — against Hamilton last season, Dundee on his debut in 1983 and Morton two years later. In February 1987, Brian scored at Tynecastle to win the *Daily Record* case of champagne as the first player to get 30 League goals. This was a repeat of his performance in 1983 when he reached the total a good deal more quickly — by three months to be exact. At the end of

February, at Dens Park, Brian grabbed his 100th League goal and this included his period with Motherwell as well as his Celtic matches. In the last Old Firm game of the season McClair stuck away two penalties and passed Charlie Nicholas's total of 29 in season 1982-83. Then at Love Street he overhauled Bobby Lennox's post-war record of League goals with his 33rd and 34th.

Winning the Golden Boot would have given Brian new status. Interestingly, three Scots have previously failed narrowly to win it. Bobby Lennox was third with 32 goals in season 1967-68, four years later Joe Harper finished in the same position with 33 and in 1982-83 Charlie Nicholas's 29 was also third best. Since McClair played so often for Celtic from the midfield his goals totals were astonishing. He was, of course, signed by Billy McNeill from Motherwell for £90,000 on 20 June 1982, and some of the £750,000 Arsenal paid for Charlie Nicholas was used. Steadily, but unspectacularly, McClair wooed the Parkhead fans until he was probably the top man. However, I don't think he wants the superstar rating which Old Trafford supporters now try to hang on him. Brian is flamboyant on the park but not off it. He has a happy family life and doesn't want it interrupted. Kenny Dalglish has much the same attitude.

Johnston had his critics but I'm not one of them. When I roomed with him on trips I found him a good guy. I took the view that if he was playing well for the team the way he ran the rest of his life was entirely his affair.

Mo went through a bad spell last season but this happens to every player. We all have off-times. Towards the end of the season, however, he came back to form but he still had a lot on his mind with all the transfer talk which culminated in him going to Nantes. Only time will tell if he made the right decision but I certainly wish him every good fortune. I think Mo has said things in newspaper articles which he has regretted. But he will have learned from these errors of judgement and will emerge the better for it. I've heard fans say Mo didn't score often enough in the really big games but my answer is to refer them to the matches which he won. And got us two points.

Like Mo, Murdo MacLeod is now earning his living abroad. I hope Murdo continues to do well. He was one of our most popular players but at 29 he got an offer from Borussia Dortmond which will make him secure for life. When the deal was going through Murdo kept the manager informed of every move and I feel this is the right way to do business.

Celtic's 1987-88 pool.
Standing: Smith, Morris, O'Leary, McKnight, Stark, McGugan, McCarthy, Bonner, Whyte, Rogan, Burns.
Sitting: McStay, Grant, Shepherd, Aitken, McGhee, Walker, Archdeacon.

Allan McInally stayed in Britain with a move to the manager's previous club, Aston Villa.

So good luck to "The Gang of Four" but now we are looking to the future with replacements who will help the club to make its mark with the club's centenary year looming. We will also, of course, be without Danny McGrain and Peter Latchford, who were given frees at the end of last season. Both were extremely popular and Danny will go into the club's history as one of the all-time greats.

Chapter 18

HOW WE LOST POINTS

MOST clubs would be quite happy to finish second top of the Premier League. But not, as I keep saying, Celtic.

We won nothing in season 1986-87 except, ironically, the trophy which Tony McGuinness donated for my testimonial match with Manchester United. Alan McInally scored the winner but victory in a friendly is not nearly enough for the Celtic legions. And so we had the sad ending of the manager, Davie Hay, being deposed.

Out of a possible 12 trophies in Davie's four-year reign, we won the Scottish Cup and the League Championship. The directors finally decided that this wasn't enough and the supporters, I have no doubt, agreed.

The players felt genuinely sad for Davie. There is simply no nice way of giving a good man the sack. I phoned him at his home to say, as team captain, how sorry we were that his management career with Celtic had ended so abruptly. However, I suppose all managers face the possibility of this happening at some point.

It was a contradictory season. The start was great. In 18 games we lost only once but, annoyingly, it was to Rangers. Our next defeat was in the Skol Cup final — to Rangers — but we then walloped Clydebank 6-0 and drew with Rangers at Parkhead. At one point we were looking so much like keeping the Championship that we were

Lou Macari's testimonial match. With Roy and Lou is the sponsor.

nine points in front of all challengers. When Graham Roberts joined Rangers we were six points ahead of them and, although Rangers had played a match fewer, he must have thought he was destined to be among the also-rans.

Alas, we threw away silly points. Whereas we had been playing as a team early in the season, we began to operate for ourselves. It wasn't premeditated. It just happened and I can't properly explain the reasons even to myself. Instead of battling for each other, self-survival became the name of the game. We began doing our own job and stopped worrying about those around us. We were happy to mind our own business, so to speak. Celtic have a cavalier style. We like to go forward and attack and entertain. There are risks attached to such a policy but I believe they are worth taking. Celtic are a good team when we've got the ball but weaker moving off it. The hardest part of our play is to pick up when we've lost possession.

Our 2-0 defeat by Rangers on New Year's Day was a body blow. We deserved to lose and there's little point in denying this. The Dinamo Kiev defeat in Russia, after drawing at Parkhead, didn't do anything for our morale either. We had to play in Russia without Tommy Burns, who was injured in the first leg. His subsequent absence from key games because of this was another factor in our disappointing season.

Despite the dejecting influence of the Kiev defeat we won our next six domestic matches but then tumbled 1-0 to Hearts in the League. Hearts turned out to be a bogey to us. That defeat should have been a Scottish Cup warning to us. Before we met at Tynecastle in the fourth round of the Cup we had just drawn 1-1 with Alex MacDonald's side. Having dismissed Aberdeen after 300 minutes — it needed a second replay after extra time in the first replay — we felt we were headed for the final at Hampden. This would have widened our trophy-winning options. However, Hearts ended our Cup run with a 1-0 victory at Tynecastle. It was a disaster.

The following week we lost 4-1 at Dens Park. It was baffling. We led at half-time and then were shooting downhill in the second half. The score was humiliating. It didn't console us at all that Rangers were out of the Cup and in even more dramatic circumstances than Celtic. They lost to Hamilton Accies at Ibrox. That must have been humbling for Graeme Souness.

In December we went to Dubai. It seemed the kind of break which would set us up nicely for the tought January programme. We drew 1-1 with Liverpool in a friendly. They scored in the last minute and then won 4-2 in a penalty shoot-out which the Arab spectators enjoyed. Our next three games were a key period. Against Motherwell, Aberdeen and Clydebank we could only draw 1-1. We should have had at least two more points out of the possible six. It was a critical bad patch. The three dropped points highlighted our inconsistency and the fact was that as a team we had lost our way. It still makes me wince when I think of these lost points.

In January I missed the 8-3 win over Hamilton and the 3-2 defeat against Dundee United. I was under SFA suspension and, although I am not excusing this, I feel that most defenders will have a ban during the season and especially as referees are being told to be strict. Nowadays a club could miss out on success because of the tough line taken by referees. The SFA would reply that this is the player's own fault. I wonder if this is completely true.

We were certainly disappointed to see our lead in the League Championship being whittled away. But I would be churlish if I didn't congratulate Rangers on their success. They will have a harder fight to keep their crown. I promise them that.

Transfer speculation during the season didn't help our cause. There is always talk in the dressing-room about new contracts but there was more of it than usual. Players heading for the end of a contact are always waiting to be called to the manager's office and have their immediate future sorted out. Mo Johnston's refusal to sign a contract caused a lot of headlines and talk. Other players wondered why he was being singled out. They wanted to have discussions as well but, when Mo's talks deadlocked, Davie Hay decided enough was enough. He said he would talk about contracts only after the final match.

This seemed to have a bad effect. It rubbed off on the team's performance. Players are like everyone else. They have mortgages to pay and family responsibilities. Footballers worry about the future, too, and if they have problems they may find it hard to concentrate. It's a difficult situation. I've been fortunate because I've always signed a new contract well in advance of the current one expiring. However, it's commonsense that a player who is worried stands a good chance of being below his best. It's the same in any job.

Our final fling was beating Rangers 3-1 in our fourth last game. There was still a chance for us to keep the title at that stage but Rangers needed to lose at least a game. However, we dropped a point to Dundee United at Parkhead and that was it. Our last game with Cup-winning St Mirren — a 3-1 win for us — was academic.

Oddly, Davie Hay's tally in four years is more than some managers can expect in a lifetime. But it wasn't good enough for Celtic and six second prizes didn't help at all. When we knew we had lost the League, everything went flat in the dressing-room. Most of the talk turned to who would stay and who wouldn't. It was soul-destroying. Being losers is not Celtic's game.

It was also a severe blow to our pockets. We are professionals. Football is our livelihood and there are big bonuses for success in the League or in cup competitions. There are no rewards for failure.

Sometimes our fans say to me they lost a tenner on a game. Naturally, we sympathise. But you can take it we've also lost about £200 in our pay packets. The supporters blame us for losing their bet for them but forget that we have a financial interest as well. However, winning is the name of our game and we have to take the consequences if we tumble.

Rangers are now the club to catch. There's certainly not much between us and I believe that Billy McNeill will ensure the gap is closed rapidly.

Disappointment over non-success, by the way, doesn't stop with the players. Men like Neil Mochan, Jim Kennedy, physio Brian Scott and that great old warhorse Jim Steele take it pretty badly too. In the dressing-room we regard them as an important part of the club team or, if you like, family, and naturally, John Kelman and Tommy Craig as well.

"Steely" is a particular character both with Celtic and Scotland. He is the joker in the pack and he's not a bad masseur, either! He has been rubbing down players at Parkhead for close on 40 years and it was Tommy Docherty who saw his potential for Scotland as masseur and funny man. I'm not sure Tommy likes a guy being funnier than him and "Steely" most certainly is.

"How much are your eggs?" asked a customer in a London Road shop. "Ninety pence a dozen but the cracked ones are half price."

"Crack me a dozen, then," said the customer.

Oops! That's the kind of jokes "Steely" makes non-stop. He has the players in fits of laughter and relaxes us completely before big matches. He has livened up the muscles of other great sportsmen, like golfer Sevvy Ballesteros and the one-time light-heavyweight champion of the world Freddie Mills. In fact, our Jim was Mills's trainer when he beat Len Harvey for the British title. "Steely" met Mills during a spell as a physical training instructor with the RAF. He looked after him for three years. When Mills jumped down from the table he would playfully aim a right then a left at "Steely". Once "Steely" forgot to duck. He got a broken nose and the fact that he did is still pretty evident to this day.

"Steely" has passed the 73 mark but he still goes out jogging most

Roy scores in the Skol Cup semi-final against Motherwell.

mornings. He believes in the good life and says this is why he remains so fit. In Scotland parties I often wonder how he keeps up his constant flow of fun. I was delighted when the Scots players handed over a painting to "Steely" during our Rous Cup matches as a small token of our appreciation. He has been on three World Cup campaigns but says he wouldn't have Andy Roxburgh's job for all the money in the world.

In fact, "Steely" has never taken a penny from Celtic. He goes to Parkhead because he loves the club and being a part of it is all the recompense he needs. For years he ran the family draper's business in Larkhall but has long since retired to his keep-fit work on himself and players like me.

On Scottish trips we are particularly fond of running race nights. These are based on edited film of races which are taken from a sealed can. Since "Steely" is the chief bookie we always feel he has a way into the seal. It may have been his unfavourable odds which prompted some of my team-mates to lift him, mattress and all, from his bed in Santa Fe where we were preparing for the Mexico World Cup finals. "Steely" was sound asleep and didn't wake up until the

Rugby at Barrowfields? No, just some fun in training with Brian Scott at the bottom of the pile. Murdo MacLeod and Roy are the "scrummers" watched by Danny McGrain.

morning, when he found a surprised foreign gentleman trying to step over him to get out of his room and into the corridor. Typical of the man "Steely" laughed louder than anyone.

Alex Ferguson and Jim McLean are two other managers who noted his skills in the art of keeping a team happy. And Graeme Souness liked him so much on Scottish trips that he hinted there would be a job for him at Ibrox if he wanted it. None of us at Parkhead needed to worry about his reply. For him to move to Ibrox would be almost as big a sensation as Paul McStay being the next Rangers captain.

When "Steely" is finished rubbing down a player he usually jokes: "Look at these muscles . . . I could play a tune on them." Celtic and Scotland have certainly been kept on song by the good humour and nimble fingers of this splendid man.

Chapter 19

SCOTLAND'S BIG PROBLEM

NO matter who manages Scotland the team will not do any better than it has done under Andy Roxburgh. The system, in which club football has priority, is geared to curb real success at international level.

Andy is unfairly criticised. He is expected to perform miracles and when he fails to do so is judged against the credentials in soccer management of the late Jock Stein. Yet even the Big Man struggled to win games at international level and he always admitted the priority naturally given to the bread and butter business of club football was crippling to Scottish elevens.

Look at the star managers who have done the Scotland job: Andy Beattie, Sir Matt Busby, Andy Beattie (second term), Ian McColl, Jock Stein, John Prentice, Malcolm MacDonald, Bobby Brown, Tommy Docherty, Willie Ormond, Ally MacLeod, Jock Stein (second term) and Alex Ferguson. Their success rate varied but certainly none succeeded as he would have liked. We have been to four successive World Cup finals, scraping in a couple of times, but never managed to get past the first round.

I say all this merely to put the position of the Scotland international team and its coach into perspective. The great expectations of the Scottish public go into the media mincing machine and emerge in a fusillade of buckshot if things go wrong. It's called partisanship. A Scottish manager has no chance, or very little, to find the all-important team blend. I have never played with the same ten players twice in the 30 internationals in which I have competed either as a substitute or for the full 90 minutes.

As captain for the six games last season I have had a closer view than most of Roxburgh's style of management. In my view he is good at the job and, given breathing space and some luck, will make a success of it.

Blend is vital in any team. Club managers can move players about from game to game until they hit on the mix that they want. But at international level key players are always unavailable for one reason or another. The coach — as Roxburgh is now called — finds his ideal line-up decimated more often than not by injuries. I doubt if Scotland have been able to play the same team twice running in living memory.

A really successful side requires a settled formation. There must be stability and this only comes with playing together. However, in Scotland club football is given the utmost priority — more so even than in England. But we still want it both ways and I feel this isn't possible.

Brazil, for instance, have already begun to tour the world preparing for the World Cup in Italy in 1990. Carlos Alberto Silva, who managed the Brazil team at Wembley and Hampden in May 1987, knows that he must produce the goods on the run-up or he won't be in Italy himself. The Brazilian FA insists that players must be released by clubs for tours to prepare them for the World Cup which they feel is more important than any club competition. This is probably why they have consistently played such a starring role in the competition.

I had to admire the carnival of genuine class football which the samba-loving Brazilians put on in beating us 2-0. The back-heels, the dummies, the 40-yard passes were spectacular, with the "unknown" Mirandinha superb in everything he did. We will hear a lot more about him. Mark my words on that.

Iron Curtain countries like the Soviet Union, Hungary and Czechoslovakia all have similar rules about the release of players for international commitments which the Football Associations of these countries feel is necessary. Italy, West Germany, Holland and Denmark are others who see the need for teams getting together to

Roy with his children John and Ashley showing strips he swopped in the World Cup

find the elusive blend and to allow the manager to be certain about options in selection to cover injuries when the chips are really down. This is the kind of fearsome backroom thinking which Andy Roxburgh has to battle against while picking his players from Scotland and England and, occasionally, farther afield.

At the moment, Scotland are a competent, hard-working side with a few inspirational players if they are able to turn it on in a particular game. It is all about what happens on the day. We are certainly not world-beaters and I've never played in a Scots side which came into that category. Probably our best set-up was around the time of the

1974 World Cup finals in West Germany when the late Willie Ormond was the manager. He had a settled team skippered by Billy Bremner and he had the luxury of reasonable continuity.

Being truly successful in Roxburgh's job is well nigh impossible. He must simply do his best with the players available and hope for a rub of the green. If Carlos Alberto, of Brazil, were to take over the same problems would still exist. Roxburgh cannot be guaranteed the players he wants when he most needs them. So quite often the team is a patch-up job. Andy puts a lot of effort into his work. I don't know anybody who could do any better. The main problems are outwith his control.

It is also wrong to argue that the international coach must be a guy who has come through the club management treadmill. The jobs are very different. A club manager is often required to look after the general running of the place as well as the team. Certainly, he would have responsibilities and more control over players than the international coach. It is not right to attempt to devalue Roxburgh because he has never managed a club. Club managers need to be experts in man management and to be able to prepare contracts, discuss wages, fix bonuses and handle directors. Roxburgh's expertise must be in coaching and handling top players mostly over a very brief period.

Andy's credentials in coaching are internationally recognised and I can tell you he has the respect of the Scottish players, including the most senior. He has been head of SFA coaching for years and the results have been steadily more impressive. I have been going to the summer coaching schemes at Largs for several years and every year the number of leading players attending has been increasing. This speaks for itself.

Roxburgh is fortunate in one aspect. He has a level-headed squad and they don't give him any hassle. Discipline can be an important factor but nobody has stepped out of line under him. Over the years this has not always been the case with other managers.

The coach is a very good organiser. Little things are attended to and the fact has not gone unnoticed among the players. For instance, we used to get our complimentary tickets when we joined the squad and then had the problem of getting them to our families. Now they are sent to our homes before we report. A little thing, I agree, but put a lot of similar items together and they become important. He does everything to keep the players happy and can still be seen to be the man with the authority.

We now get a strip to wear and another to give away if we want. He knows the number of times players are asked for their jerseys. The one I wore at Hampden against Brazil is either in Rio or in Newcastle. Mirandinha took it. Similarly, every Scots player now has personal cards to give out to supporters. On them are his picture and a pen portrait. This will help the public as well.

Eventually, there will be a spin-off from Roxburgh's work if he is given time. The Tartan Army shouldn't look for too much too soon.

I have to be frank. I don't believe Scotland have enough class players. Certainly not as many as the fans seem to think. Certain other countries seem better at bringing youngsters through . . . better than Scotland, although I have already explained some of the difficulties. Roxburgh can't go into the transfer market to solve his problems. He has to make do with what the clubs provide for him.

Andy is now determined to play to a 4-4-2 system. This could be the start of something good. Although its application can be varied slightly the players will at least have consistency in the style of the team. Jackie Charlton's Republic of Ireland use this plan very well and so at club level do Dundee United. It's maybe worth recalling that Eire beat Brazil 1-0 in a friendly in May with a goal scored by Liam Brady. Charlton is lucky to have two players, Tony Galvin and Ray Houghton, who are particularly good in the wide midfield positions, just as Eamonn Bannon is for United.

Scotland's biggest failing is an inability to score. It is much more difficult to get goals at international level because of the quickness and skills of defenders. Brian McClair scored 41 goals for Celtic last season and Ally McCoist got 35 for Rangers but when Roxburgh sat down to pick his side against Hungary in September he had to be mindful of the fact that neither player has beaten a goalie while wearing a dark blue jersey.

The lack of goals by Scotland, which goes back a lot of years, underlines the gulf between international and club football. Although Scots players find themselves with more time on the ball at the highest level the pace of play is also much quicker and more decisive once in the last third of the park. Brazil showed us how to do it in the Rous Cup. Their build-up was slow but when they got into the danger area they suddenly became electric. It was like turning on a switch. We can't seem to get that kind of team understanding and are one-paced throughout games.

Nor are Scots fans geared to that style of play although they like it from the Brazilians. They want us to go at 100 mph all the time. In that game at Hampden if Brazil passed back they were cheered. If we did the same the crowd booed us. Perhaps we would be better to settle for a big man up front and use him as a target man. Get the ball up to him as we once did with Joe Jordan.

The last Scotland-England game attracted a lot of criticism. And this although a scoreless game was a better result for us than England. Once again the Scots team had been decimated and even our most loyal fans thought we were for it. Frankly, we went out to make sure England couldn't play as they wanted. They didn't do much but at the end of the day neither did we. Roxburgh was pleased, however, that we stemmed the dangers of Glenn Hoddle, Bryan Robson and Chris Waddle. I would like to have seen us doing better though. A pity that a shot by Charlie Nicholas rattled off the crossbar when he came on in the second half. Six inches down and it was a goal because Chris Woods was beaten.

In the Brazil game we had more scope because they stood away from us. Tackling, toughly that is, isn't really their style although they can indulge in it if required. They made the game longer for us by the clever way they retreated, pulling us back and then striking forward like Allan Wells in football boots.

I don't think we could ever play like the Brazilians. Even if we could the fans wouldn't let us pass the ball around at the back as they do. They also have a natural athleticism which Scots don't have. Some of it comes from playing on the beaches of Brazil as wee lads. Brazil's build-up would be too slow for our fans. They are not used to this and wouldn't have the patience. I recall Graeme Souness saying that Scots never understood it was necessary to go back at times to get forward. If we try passing between us at the back we get a raspberry from the Hampden terracings. They want a charge of the heavy brigade. All the time.

I've been selected by four international team bosses — Ally MacLeod, Jock Stein, Alex Ferguson and Andy Roxburgh. I didn't actually get on the park in Ally's time but very nearly did for the last ten minutes in Austria. My first appearance was against Peru at Hampden. Jock Stein sent me on for the last 20 minutes. We drew 1-1. It was a great experience. Peru were a good side to play against for the first time in a Scots jersey.

The game I remember most was in Belgium when they beat us 3-2 and Kenny Dalglish scored twice. Scotland played really well against a country who are among the most highly rated. Frank Gray missed a penalty in the last minute for us. This would have meant a draw had he been successful and even Guy Thys, the veteran Belgian manager, said we had deserved this.

Kenny scored first, Belgium levelled and Kenny made it 2-1. Dalglish scored a goal that night which is one of the best I have ever seen. He came from the right, cut in and screwed it with his left foot into the far corner. It was a world-class goal from a world-class player.

Moving into the top Scotland squad wasn't so hard for me as I had come through every grade. And quite a few of the players with whom I took part at under-21 level were by that time in the full squad as well. I went into the international arena when Billy McNeill was in charge. We had won a couple of championships and Celtic were doing well. So I felt good about being picked for my country.

Let me underline that to play for Scotland is a tremendous honour. I would do it for nothing. The fee we get is an incidental. And I can say emphatically that this goes for all the players I've ever been with in a Scotland group. This is one area where "playing for the jersey" still counts.

Roy's Record

International honours:	30 full caps and honoured at all levels from schoolboy under-15s.
Club honours:	Five Championship medals, three Scottish Cup winners medals, one League Cup winners medal.
Total games for Celtic to the end of season 1986-87:	556
First appearance in Celtic's top team:	League Cup quarter-final at Stenhousemuir, 10 September 1975, second-half substitute (Bobby Lennox and Kenny Dalglish scored).
First League appearance:	Pittodrie, 21 February 1976 (Bobby Lennox scored 79th-minute winner)

CUP FINALS

	Competition	*Opponents*	*Score* (Celtic first)
1976/77	League	Aberdeen	1-2
	Scottish	Rangers	1-0
1977/78	League	Rangers	1-2 (after extra time)
1979/80	Scottish	Rangers	1-0 (after extra time)
1982/83	League	Rangers	2-1
1983/84	League	Rangers	2-3 (after extra time)
	Scottish	Aberdeen	1-2 (after extra time)
1984/85	Scottish	Dundee United	2-1
1986/87	League (Skol)	Rangers	1-2

EUROPEAN MATCHES

Season	*Competition*	*Opposition*	*Scores* (Celtic first)	*Aggregate*
1975-76	E.C.¼f	Sachsenring Zwickau	1-1 0-1	1-2
1976-77	UEFA f.r.	Wislaw Krakow	†2-2 0-2	2-4
1977-78	E.C. f.r.	Jeunesse d'Esch	5-0 6-1	11-1
	s.r.	SWW Innsbruck	2-1 0-3	2-4
1979-80	E.C. f.r.	Partizan Tirana	0-1 4-1	4-2
	s.r.	Dundalk	3-2 0-0	3-2
	¼f	Real Madrid	2-0 0-3	2-3
1980-81	C.W.C. f.r.	Diosgyeori Politechnica	6-0 1-2	7-2
	s.r.	Timisoara	2-1 0-1	2-2 (Celts lost on away goal)
1981-82	E.C. f.r.	Juventus	1-0 0-2	1-2
1982-83	E.C. f.r.	Ajax	†2-2 2-1	4-3
	s.r.	Real Sociedad	0-2 2-1	2-3
1983-84	UEFA f.r.	Aarhus	1-0 4-1	5-1
	s.r.	Sporting Lisbon	0-2 5-0	5-2
	¼f	Nottingham F	0-0 1-2	1-2
1984-85	C.W.C. f.r.	KAA Ghent	0-1 3-0	3-1
	s.r.	Vienna Rapid	1-3 3-0* 0-1	1-4
1985-86	C.W.C. f.r.	Atletico Madrid	1-1 1-2	2-3
1986-87	E.C. f.r.	Shamrock Rovers	1-0 2-0	3-0
	s.r.	Dinamo Kiev	1-1 1-3	2-4

† Roy didn't play in first tie

* This result didn't count in aggregate score

OLD FIRM APPEARANCES

Year	*Games*	*Goals*
1975/76	1	0
1976/77	4	2
1977/78	4	0
1978/79	5	1
1979/80	5	0
1980/81	4	1

1981/82	4	0
1982/83	4	0
1983/84	3	1
1984/85	4	0
1985/86	4	0
1986/87	5	1

Played 47 Scored 6 Won 21 Lost 11 Drawn 15

SCOTLAND APPEARANCES

Scotland v Peru	1-1	1979/80	(sub for 20 minutes)
Scotland v Belgium	1-3	1979/80	(Full Game)
Scotland v England	0-2	1979/80	(Full Game)
Poland v Scotland	1-0	1979/80	(Full Game)
Scotland v Wales	1-0	1979/80	(Sub for ten minutes)
Belgium v Scotland	3-2	1982/83	(Full Game)
Canada v Scotland	0-2	1982/83	(Sub for 30 minutes)
Canada v Scotland	0-3	1982/83	(Full Game)
Scotland v Uruguay	1-1	1983/84	(Sub for 15 minutes)
N. Ireland v Scotland	2-0	1983-84	(Full Game)
Scotland v Wales	2-1	1983/84	(Sub for 20 minutes)
Scotland v England	1-0	1984/85	(Full Game)
Iceland v Scotland	0-1	1984/85	(Full Game)
Wales v Scotland	0-1	1985/86	(Full Game)
Scotland v East Germany	0-0	1985/86	(Full Game)
Scotland v Australia	2-0	1985/86	(Full Game)
Australia v Scotland	0-0	1985/86	(Full Game)
Israel v Scotland	0-1	1985/86	(Full Game)
Scotland v Rumania	3-0	1985/86	(Full Game & First Goal)
England v Scotland	2-1	1985/86	(Full Game)

WORLD CUP GAMES — Mexico

Scotland v Denmark	0-1		(Full Game)
Scotland v West Germany	1-2		(Full Game)
Scotland v Uruguay	0-0		(Full Game)

Scotland v Bulgaria	0-0	1986/87	(Full Game)
Eire v Scotland	0-0	1986/87	(Full Game — Captain)

Scotland v Luxembourg	3-0	1986/87	(Full Game — Captain)
Scotland v Eire	0-1	1986/87	(Full Game — Captain)
Belgium v Scotland	1-4	1986/87	(Full Game — Captain)
Scotland v England	0-0	1986/87	(Full Game — Captain)
Scotland v Brazil	0-2	1986/87	(Full Game — Captain)